THE RANGE OF REALITY

(THE SECRET OF UFOS)

By Ray Holm

PublishAmerica
Baltimore

First printing

ISBN: 1-4137-5878-9
PUBLISHED BY PUBLISHAMERICA, LLLP
www.publishamerica.com
Baltimore

Printed in the United States of America

DEDICATION

This book is dedicated to all people who have observed UFOs, been abducted by aliens or government agencies, who believe in extraterrestrial beings, who doubt government explanations of UFOs, or who simply understand that there is a force and intelligence out there which is greater than understood or accepted by many today.

ACKNOWLEDGMENTS

I could never have completed this book without the support and encouragement given me by my family and friends.

My special thanks to my wife, Dawn, for the contributions, patience and insights she gave. She is blessed with true psychic abilities, and has had her own experiences with phenomena not generally accepted by traditional scientific theory. She has the gift to speak with and see spirits. She has the gift to travel and remote view. She has spoken with, and seen, Jesus Christ the Lord, and God. She has pushed me through my moments of doubt when I was reluctant to continue writing because of possible ridicule that may come upon the family. She said, "We can handle it."

Dustin, our 16-year-old son, was always at my side to insure peace and quiet while I was busy and to make sure I got enough rest. Dustin also has the gift of speaking with and seeing spirits. He is quite psychic, but likes to keep it to himself. There are two angel friend who hang around him, and are visible to others at times. He has no fear of this, and states that everyone has an angel or two. He is truly an animal lover and knows they have spirits.

Christina (Xenia Christiane) Piroska, a world-renowned dancer, singer and psychic with a circle of wonderful friends, I thank you for being our friend and sharing your insights.

I thank Richard and Kate Mucci, the handsome couple who host the well-known and expanding TV show, *Out There*, which originates from Pahrump, Nevada, and is aired in many parts of the U.S and internationally, for their shared knowledge and insights. Also, I thank them for their mighty patience while I wrote this book and their very helpful contributions. *Out There* is a breath of fresh air for all those who believe in, or are curious about, aliens, UFOs and other phenomena. The show's guests are talented, knowledgeable and informative.

Garth and Kevin Farrington-House: Garth is a well know psychic who has fought hard for the preservation of the credibility of true psychics. He has assisted many people throughout the world to recover funds given to frauds posing as psychics. Kevin, who is truly spiritual, has a deep and wonderful appreciation for the love and nature of all animals.

Ginger and Gary Thompson, who have given their unselfish encouragement and points of view based on their own experiences of contacts from the unknown.

There are many others I have not mentioned here, who gave me encouragement and information, but I have you in my heart and prayers.

CONTENTS

PREFACE

I did not want to write this book. It is with great trepidation that I did so. I was contacted by aliens, first by the feeling of a "presence" around me which then became a "voice," and then they made themselves visible to me. Their purpose was to give me a "Mission" to perform for them. I have been directed to write this book by those extraterrestrial beings as a part of that "Mission" which I agreed to perform. It sounded like a simple task, at first.

They have directed that I write of the teachings they have given me, the experiences I have had with them, as well as some of the experiences of others. They have given me much information and some special "gifts" and insights, but with a caveat that I may only divulge that which they authorize. I cannot change the meaning of anything they have directed me to write. They speak to me telepathically, but are visible at the time of these communications.

Are UFOs and extraterrestrial beings real or imaginary? Is there a dividing line between reality and what is called supernatural? Just what that is, is up to each of us to determine. Is it a sharp and clear division or is it all a gray area?

I believe it is all the same. There is no dividing line between reality and the supernatural. We live in a world that folds our three-dimensional environment neatly into all of those other dimensions that we have a feeling are there but cannot define scientifically. However, I do know there is a dividing line in the realm of our souls as humans on Earth. It is the line between positive and negative, sometimes called good and evil. That line is visible to me. We each have one. The ability for me to see that line is one of the "gifts" given to me by the extraterrestrial beings.

Throughout history, mankind has been reluctant to change thinking of life and the universe as it had been taught. Those who dare step forward are generally met with severe ridicule and rejection. Over 2,000 years ago, Socrates was ridiculed and rejected because of his teachings of a question-and-answer philosophy that taught people to think for themselves. Galileo was imprisoned during the Inquisition for advocating a heliocentric theory (the sun is the center of our solar system) about 450 years ago.

Daily our lives are changing because new discoveries are proving that concepts held as absolutes are defective. At one time, when the telegraph was patented, the director of the United States Patent and Trademark Office advised the president that he could now close the Patent and Trademark Office because everything that could be invented had been. There were no more inventions which could be made, he blabbered on. His position protected him from public ridicule. Thank heaven that we still have free-thinking people who are brave enough to speak out, knowing they may incur ridicule and scorn.

I have had experiences with UFOs and extraterrestrial beings. I know there is a God. I know there are ghosts, spirits, angels and souls, some good and some evil. I know there is a Satan, for I have seen his face. I know there are other dimensions, because I have experienced them. And all of those are the reasons I am writing this book.

I have been told by these extraterrestrial beings that every human has a soul, and every animal has a soul.

In this book I am not attempting to change anyone's point of view or beliefs. Nor is it about religion or politics, even though it has a spiritual message for all humans. It is about extraterrestrial beings, the supernatural and unidentified flying objects. It may seem to some that I am opinionated and may even be making derogatory statements about some people, religions, and politics. But that is not my intention. I am writing what I have been directed to write, and in the form I have been directed to follow. I make no judgments about people or organizations. In the exercise of my free will, I appreciate any criticism of my point of view by others who are likewise exercising their free will.

I was promised that no harm would come to me while performing this "Mission." However, they did inform me that I would go through many trials and hardships, and must not grow impatient or waiver from the purpose of my "Mission." They told me that I would encounter resistance from sources outside this dimension we are in, from powerful forces that are totally negative and do not want this "Mission" completed or its message heard. Little did I know at that time just how powerful those negative forces are, or the hardships I would encounter.

CHAPTER 1
THE "PRESENCE"

A feeling, an awareness of a presence, had been with me for a long time. I could not see it, touch it or explain it. It seemed to be always there with me – right beside me. I had often thought it just might be only my imagination. At least that is what I was hoping it was. However, I knew deep in my soul that it was more than that. But just what was it? There was never any interference from the presence with what I was doing. There was no harm or frightening experiences. I had no fear of it, but its constant presence was quite bothersome. I kept this to myself. I told no one about it. I was afraid to tell anyone about it because I was certain that I would be ridiculed for having such feelings.

As time passed I got the feeling there was something I was supposed to do. The presence made me feel that way. I would ask myself, *But what could that be? Have I forgotten something important? Am I about to lose my job? Is this an omen of something that is going to happen, such as an earthquake or nuclear war or a devastating storm or some major disaster? Am I going to be injured or, worse yet, killed?* All of those thoughts and more crossed my mind every time I thought of that "presence."

I had no idea from what source this presence was emanating, but I did realize it was real and at the same time I had doubts. At first I inquired of certain friends and acquaintances about their beliefs in ghosts and spirits. I asked in a vague manner if they could feel their presence. I was generally told that there were no such things, that spirits and ghosts were related to some church or religion and were just bunk. I asked these friends and acquaintances if they ever felt like they had a spirit or ghost hanging around them, and again the responses were negative or noncommittal. Some said that if they ever had such an experience they would not tell anyone about it, which sounded like something I should do.

When I was growing up, I was always curious about the vastness of our universe. It seemed to me that there must be more out there than what I was aware of here on Earth. This vast universe appears to be orderly by its nature. It is consistent even during change. Life must be that way also. I wondered just why we were here. Did we have a purpose? Were we just an accident? Where did the first atom originate and who or what created it? Are more being created? If not, would creation stop and simply fade away? There are all kinds of theories. I had no idea what was waiting for me in the future!

CHAPTER 2
MY FIRST UFO ENCOUNTER

My first encounter with UFOs came one day when a business associate and I had driven from Palm Springs, California, to the west side of Mt. San Jacinto, where we were scouting around for a potential site for a real estate development. We located a beautiful meadow sparsely populated by tall pine trees. As we were driving on a dirt road through this area, we were startled to see three disc-shaped objects ahead of us and to our left, slowly moving parallel to us through the tall pines. They were about 30 feet above the ground.

Startled, my friend stopped the vehicle and we just sat there looking at those objects for a moment. We exited and stood starring is disbelief. I had never seen anything like that before. They moved slowly along at the same speed, and there was absolutely no sound emanating from them, at least no sound that we could hear. The only sound was from the engine in our vehicle. They moved past us with still no sound at all.

These objects appeared to be about 30 to 60 feet in diameter. There were no lights on them. There were no visible windows or doors. As they methodically moved past us, they made no threatening moves. It was as though we did not exist to them. I cannot be sure, because it was like time was frozen, but I think they were visible to us for about three minutes. Then they vanished.

It seemed to me that they simultaneously made a little upward movement and simply disappeared. They did not accelerate. There was no whoosh of air or blast from an exhaust. They just vanished.

Now it was as though they had never been there. It was all quiet and weird. We certainly were not the object of their presence in that area. They made no indication that they were even aware of us being there. They posed no threat, and we felt no danger.

When I first saw these objects I thought they must be balloons or some aerobatics team practicing some maneuver. But there were no ropes or lines hanging down from them. At the time, it never occurred to me that they might be part of some military exercise, but I thought of that later.

My friend and I got back into the vehicle and sat silently for a few moments. We discussed what we had witnessed. He, as well as myself, were quite disturbed by this event. We had observed objects that no one could identify or explain. We concurred that what we had just seen was the same for both of us. We had seen the same thing.

We drove back to Palm Springs and only talked sporadically. We agreed that we had seen flying saucers. They were shaped like saucers. The bottoms were flat and the top was slightly rounded. They looked exactly alike.

My friend was very agitated and uneasy about this event. He told me that he was never going to mention this to anyone, because he had a business reputation to protect. He was quite emphatic about this, and informed me that if I should ever mention it to anyone, I was not to mention his name. He told me several times on our way back to Palm Springs that he would deny any knowledge of such an event, and I would be on my own if I should mention it. He seemed angry with me, as though this was all my fault. I promised him I would not mention his name if I ever told anyone about it. I had no intention of telling anyone about it because I realized people would ridicule me if I did so.

When we got back to Palm Springs we did not return to his office. We parted ways and I never saw him again. We had been friends for several years, but after that incident, he did not take my phone calls when I called his office, and he never called me. I received word that he has since passed away. I never told anyone about this incident while he was alive.

CHAPTER 3
THE "VOICE"

Time passed but the feeling of a presence near me would not go away as I had hoped. It seemed to be getting stronger. I was now living and working in North Carolina. One morning while driving to work, this "presence" came upon me so powerfully it frightened me. I could feel it all around me. It was like a static field building up. I kept driving. There was no communication by me or from that very strong "presence."

Then the "presence" took on a human form, standing on a wide ledge, high on a mountainside. Behind the presence was a high cliff and at the base of the cliff there was a mist-shrouded, cave-like entrance to which the presence was motioning for me to either enter or look into. I peered into the cave but there was nothing there that I could see. I did not enter.

This apparition lasted only momentarily. It disappeared as quickly as it appeared. This did not interfere with my driving. The image was a man standing with a shepherd's staff held vertically in one hand and motioning with the other. He had long hair and was dressed in a long off-white robe. During the entire duration of this vision, I was in full control of the vehicle, and could clearly see the roadway. I admit I was shaken by this encounter, but at the same time I found a form of relief in the fact that there was a physical appearance associated with the "presence" and that I had not lost my mind.

It was clear to me that I had felt the "presence" get stronger and stronger as I was driving. It just kept building until it manifested itself in that vision. I knew now that there was a lot more to this feeling of some "presence" always being around me – it has now taken on a more personal contact. It had actually contacted me in this manner for some reason, but I was unable to figure out what possible reason it could be. But I knew that something had changed and would never be the same again. I just did not realize what was in store for me. I soon arrived at work, but confided this to no one.

A few weeks passed, and this encounter was on my mind many times. At work, at home, and while trying to go to sleep at night, I constantly attempted to sort this all out. It was impossible to do so. It was not logical – it was not scientific – and I had always considered myself to be both. Since I had seen the apparition, the feeling of the constant "presence" was gone. I did not know what was going on now, because this was the first time that I can recall that I did not have that feeling of the "presence" hanging around. I thought that maybe seeing the apparition took care of the problem.

Weeks passed without the "presence" or the apparition manifesting themselves to me, so at church one day, I decided to relate this experience to a lady I thought was understanding about such matters. I thought that perhaps she would be able to explain what my vision meant. I knew she was a devout and dedicated Christian who was very active in church activities. So after services concluded, I approached and requested we meet outside to discuss this matter.

She readily agreed, and we proceeded to the front of the church, whereupon I related the experience I had had with the apparition. She responded, "It was Jesus Christ, The Lord." I had not expected that response. It took me back a little. I thought on that for a moment. She asked me to describe him. I replied that I could not, but really I did not want to get into that. She asked, "Did you see his face? Tell me what he looks like." She was quite excited, and had already made up her mind about the vision.

I responded by saying, "My understanding and knowledge is that no one has ever looked upon the face of God. I am certain this was not the Lord Jesus Christ, and I had the feeling it was not. It was the apparition of a being, but not of God or Jesus Christ." I broke away from this conversation as quickly as possible because it was going into an arena which I did not want to get into, at least at this time. I vowed then that I would never discuss this with anyone, as there was undoubtedly no one to really talk to that I knew of.

More weeks passed, but there was no presence and there were no more incidents. Then one day, as I was doing some yard work at my home, the "presence" came upon me again. It was back. I could feel it all around me. I wondered what was going to happen now. It was very strong. It became so powerful that I could not move. I was frozen, but not fearful. I stood transfixed, rake in hand. There was nothing near me, but I felt as though it was all around me, close. It was like static electricity. There was no doubt in my mind it had returned. *But why?* I asked myself. I had nothing to offer. I knew it was there, as I could feel it as surely as I felt the rake in my hands. I recalled the incident while on my way to work when the apparition made itself visible to me and wondered if I was about to have another similar experience. I looked around me. There was nothing there but lawn, trees, and plants. There was no one and there was no visible apparition. I knew it was there. I just could not see it.

Then came to my mind (whether I could hear it, or was it telepathy, I do not know) a message, "I am here, but you cannot see nor hear me." Then silence for what seemed to be an eternity. I waited—I really did not have a choice. There was nothing I could do. I thought, *Why so long?* I knew I had been spoken to, but there was no one around. *Was this all just in my mind?* I thought to myself. How can there be verbal communication but no sound? That is impossible. It must have been telepathic, if there was anything at all.

But I could hear the voice as clearly as I can hear the call to dinner. When I hear that call, I go to dinner. It did not feel as though there was sound. I felt quite certain that this was a communication from the "presence" directly to my mind. It was from a power outside my body directly to my mind. I could tell, but I cannot explain to anyone else, unless they have had a similar experience.

After this wait, which seemed like hours but was probably only seconds (because I noticed the grass in the lawn had not grown during this seemingly long wait), came the "voice" loud and resonant, but calming and soft at the same time, "I am here, but you cannot see nor can you hear me. There is a mission for you to perform. There are things which shall occur before you will be given direction. These are the things which shall happen directly to you. Do not question this direction. You will have no control over what takes place or when it will happen. First, you will be bitten by a poisonous snake. It will not be a fatal bite. Do not worry about it, for on the fifth day you will completely recover. Second, you will be burned in a fire. The burns shall not be fatal, and will leave no scars. You will completely recover in nine days. You shall then relocate to a desert area. You will know when you are there, for I shall tell you. I will make a sign, and you will know you are there, for you shall know the sign when you receive it. You will then wait in the desert area for my further instructions and directions. You must not grow inpatient. Do not doubt that I will be there with you, for I shall be there. You shall work and conduct your ordinary life. When it is time for me to meet you, I shall contact you and give you your instructions and directions."

Suddenly, I was alone. The "voice" was gone. As quickly as it came upon me, it was gone. I use the expression "came upon me" because I know of no other way to say it. While it was speaking, I could not move. It had actually taken control of me, but in a peaceful manner. I wanted to ask questions, but there was no one to ask. I was frozen, and probably could not have said anything if I had had the opportunity.

I no longer felt that the "voice" was around me. I did not feel a presence. I felt that no harm had come to me, but what about all of the things that were to happen to me? Again I asked myself, *Why me?* I have no political, economic or religious influence. I had many questions to ask this "voice," this "presence" which, uninvited, had suddenly intruded into my life and being. I felt I had a right to know. I had not stood on a mountaintop with arms raised, chanting for some mysterious "presence" to take control of my life.

I thought to myself, *I had better get back to reality. This is impossible. There was no one there. It was just my imagination, and that strong authoritative "voice" was only a figment of my imagination.* I realized that there was no particular spot from which the "voice" emanated. It had just been all around me, like surround-sound. No human can do that.

I came out of my "frozen state" and began to relax a little. This was pretty unnerving, even though I was not afraid. I returned to my yard work, but was oblivious to what I was doing. I could have been using the wrong end of the rake, and not known the difference between that and the correct side. As I puttered around, I felt more traumatized. If it wasn't trauma then it was just a notch above total confusion, with a portion of resentment thrown in. I probably destroyed half a dozen daisies before I realized I could not concentrate. I noticed my nervousness when I looked at my trembling hands. I held them out in front of me and tried to quiet them. No go. I had enough of this for the day. I retreated into the house and poured a cup of hot coffee, then sat down at the kitchen table. Thank heaven I was home alone so I didn't have to explain my demeanor to anyone.

The coffee was hot and tasted good. I thought I could now relax and get this thing out of my mind, but that didn't work. It was becoming all-consuming. I resolved while sitting there that the only solution to this was to get it out of my mind and keep it out. I said aloud, "Put it aside. Forget it." I was alone and thought to myself, *Now I am beginning to talk to myself. That yard work can wait for some other day.*

Like all things, it is much easier said than done to put things out of your mind or forget them. I found I could not get them out of my mind for even a second. Every word "spoken" to me was clearly impressed in my mind as though I was reading it from a tablet. It played through my mind as though I was hearing it again and again. I was not hearing it though, it was just impressed into my mind.

As the days went by I wondered why I would be contacted by something like this. I knew it was real. I knew it was an actual being of some kind. I was not imagining this. I was sure I was not imagining because I could hear it so clearly and could feel the "presence." Right now there was no "presence." It seemed to come to me only just before it made contact. I knew it was an actual contact and was certain it was some form of extraterrestrial being. No human could do that. But why would I, just an average person, be contacted and informed that I was going to perform a "mission," and further, that I would have no control over it?

Why wouldn't they go to Art Bell, the president of the United States, the Pentagon, Donald Trump, or some individual with influence to perform a "mission," whatever it was going to be? There are those who have clairvoyant powers and experience with the spirit world, and those who have had experiences with occupants of UFOs—why not them? In my case, there was no UFO perched in my yard, no whir, whoosh or other dramatic arrival and departure—just the feeling of the "presence" just before the "voice" became audible, said its piece, and then left me to myself.

Now the thought came to me that I should share this experience with others. But with whom? The newspaper, TV station, radio station or a religious group? I had better give this notion some serious review before doing it. What good would it do, and who would even be interested, anyway? I came to the conclusion that if I went to anyone with this event, I would be branded a kook so fast it would make your head swim. I had no proof of the existence of this thing.

The conventional scientific community, as well as religious groups, would require proof of some kind. I had absolutely none, just the recollection of the apparition and the "voice" that spoke to me. In my own way of thinking, I felt that the "voice" had so much power that it could control the world with "words." It has the power to make me stop and listen to it whether I like it or not, and whenever and wherever it so desires. I had no control. After my encounter, I realized I was quite frightened and bewildered. I hoped I would never have another encounter with it and that this was all my imagination. I decided to keep this to myself and tell no one, to never mention it to anyone at any time. I also had a deeper appreciation for my friend's fears when we encountered the three UFOs near Palm Springs.

I began thinking about the content of the message I was given by the "voice," and what it could mean. It said I would be bitten by a poisonous snake, but it would not be fatal. Well, there certainly are enough poisonous snakes in North Carolina. They are no real threat to anyone unless a person gets careless or unlucky. I do not like snakes, and if there is one within a mile of me, I won't be in that neighborhood very long. How would I be bitten if I was careful, which I already was?

I lived in an old, magnificent-looking, 4,000-square-foot brick house sitting on five wooded acres with two creeks intersecting it. This wooded environment, as well as that of all of the other similar adjoining properties, created an attractive habitat for many birds, snakes and wild animals. There were rattlesnakes, copperheads, cottonmouth moccasins and others that were not venomous. Deer and bears were frequent visitors. There were many possums and raccoons. I had seen quite a few snakes and snapping turtles in that area and was always cautious while near the brush by the creek banks. I was pretty certain that "event" was not going to happen.

Next, there was to be a fire at which I was to be a guest. I could not foresee me at a fire. I avoid such things. There are firemen who are very good at handling those situations, and I am not needed. I could see no way that this event was going to happen.

Then I was to relocate to a desert and wait there for further instructions. I did not want to live in the desert. They are hot, windy and dusty. I did not have any desire to move from a semi-swamp area to a hot, arid desert, the nearest which would be about a thousand miles away. This was not going to happen, either. It was not on my agenda, and I had no intention of putting it there.

In my mind, I felt pretty sure I had properly resolved these matters. None of these events would take place. I thought to myself that nothing like this can happen. It is not real. My rationale was that if you cannot see it, it's not there. If it's not there, it can't talk. If it can't talk, then nothing really happened. That seemed quite logical to me.

CHAPTER 4
THE EVENTS

Days had now passed since my last encounter with the "voice." Nothing had happened and no visitation or incidents occurred. The days turned into months and the impressions I had received from the "presence" and the "voice" were becoming distant memories in my mind. I was now thinking about this only on rare occasions. I was in my normal routine and nothing had disrupted it. This made me feel pretty good.

I was walking around the front yard admiring the cherry trees just coming into bloom. The azaleas and camellias were about to burst into full bloom also. There were some daffodils and narcissus blooming. All in all, it was a most pleasant moment. This, in my estimation, was always the most pleasant time of year.

It was about then that I noticed the lawn needed mowing. This would be a good time to do that, so I went to the utility shed and got the lawnmower, wheelbarrow and rakes. As twigs, leaves and pine nettles from the pecan, pine, oak and maple trees had littered the yard, I decided to rake them up before mowing. It was past the time of year for frost so it was also time to remove the pine straw from around the base of the azaleas planted in beds around the house. The lawn took up over one acre so it was not going to be a quick and easy task.

I recruited some help to get this done. We raked the twigs and pine straw from the yard and the base of the azaleas onto the edge of the lawn. Now it was time to begin loading these large piles of leaves, branches and twigs onto the wheelbarrow and take them to the burn pile. It was also getting around noon so we decided to have lunch.

After lunch we returned to the task of loading and hauling the piles of debris from the yard. I warned my helper that when picking up piles of debris one should be careful, as there may be a snake hiding in there. They do this hunting for rodents and other things they eat. I demonstrated that before picking up a pile, one should take the rake and shake and move the pile around, and hopefully, this would frighten any snake out and away. I felt it was safe to pick up, so I reached down and put my hands around a bunch of twigs and pine straw and began lifting it. At that moment there was a quick, sharp hit on my ring finger. It stung a little. I jumped back looking at my finger. There were two small round marks on the outside of the lower finger joint. It felt like a twig had snapped against my finger. I took the rake and moved the pile out flat and raked through it several times to see if there was a snake in it. I could not find a snake. It must have escaped while I was looking at my hand. It would be simple for the snake to get away as the pile was at the edge of the lawn and up against the brushy area of the property. I never saw it.

When I was first struck by the snake I presumed it was a twig that had snapped against my hand when I picked up the pile of debris. After the hit on my finger and the fact that I could not find a snake in the pile, I was sure that it had just been some sharp thorns or splintered end of a twig that made the marks. I went to the utility shed and brought back a pitchfork to pick up the piles, no longer using my bare hands. By the time we had completed the yard work, my finger was stinging pretty good. It was throbbing and the hand was beginning to discolor. Within four hours the discoloration was quite severe.

There was a lot of pain in the finger now and I got a terrible headache. I knew that it had been a snake, but I had not seen it and did not know what kind it was. It was about time to seek some medical attention.

I called a hospital emergency room and was put in contact with a person who was the snakebite expert. He was not a doctor. I was told to look for the puncture wounds and describe them to the expert. As these were really easy to locate, I did that. He inquired if I could describe the bite marks, as he was certain it was a snake bite. After I gave him the description, he requested that I contact a hospital and get there as quickly as I could. I talked to him a while longer and asked him exactly what the treatment would be for this. He then told me they would only observe me, because the anti-venom serum, if not specifically for this type snake, would react as though I had been bitten by another snake.

I did not go to the hospital, but kept ice packs on the bite. At one time, I had been told by a man that if one should be bitten by a poisonous snake, there was a treatment (or home remedy, if one wishes), which is to drink lots of whole milk and egg whites. I began to do that. I did not want to go a hospital and have a bunch of people charge me huge bucks to stand around and look at me helplessly while piling up a huge bill. All they could do would be give me some kind of pain killer, but as far as that is concerned, I wasn't interested. I could handle the discomfort – I wanted a cure and they didn't have one.

I continued my home-remedy treatment program. By the next day, my hand was very swollen and had taken on a light purple-bluish color. My head ached terribly. For the next five days I stayed in bed and drank enough eggnog to supply Christmas drinks to the entire population of a small community. I ate aspirin and kept my hand covered with ice packs.

It was late in the afternoon of the fifth day that I got my first relief. I had gotten up and was sitting in the kitchen at the table, when as suddenly as a curtain being raised, my headache completely subsided and the pain in my hand ceased. It left so quickly I could not believe it. I sat stunned for a few minutes waiting for it to return.

But it did not come back. The swelling and discoloration were the same, though. I sat up for about four hours and then went back to bed. The next morning when I awoke and looked at my hand, the swelling and discoloration were all but gone. Two days later there was nothing to remind me of this except my memory and the two small fang marks on the lower joint of my ring finger.

During my mini-vacation in bed, I gave serious thought to the prophecies of the "voice" that I would be bitten by a poisonous snake and recover on the fifth day. This is exactly what had happened. I felt that this whole incident would be better chalked up to coincidence and negligence rather than a prediction by a mysterious "voice." This was reasonable as far as I was concerned, but to discount the event was not that simple. It was back on my mind constantly again, and I thought of the prediction of being burned in a fire. The "voice" or "presence" had not been with me since the prediction was made and were not around me now.

It was now in the mid-fall season when the leaves from the trees had all fallen. I was completely recovered from the snakebite, both mentally and physically, but still had the occasional thought of the bout with the snake. I was back again raking leaves and debris, determined I would no longer reach into stacks of leaves and twigs with my hands. I got out my wheelbarrow, rakes, and pitchfork and was ready to tackle the task. I hoped all of the snakes would be in hibernation as the weather was now quite cold. *I will have to do this again in the spring,* I thought to myself as I began work.

There was a clearing among the trees about 300 feet from the house where I burned the leaves, twigs, small limbs, and any other thing of wood or paper. I raked the yard and took all of the debris to the burn pile. I also collected many other tree limbs and debris left from a recent hurricane and its tornados. It was a pretty good-sized pile when I completed that task. I looked around and was pleased that the yard looked much better, but there was one other thing I had intended to do for some time now, and this would be the perfect time to do it.

There was a small, dilapidated, old storage building at the back of the property which, as far as I was concerned, was an eyesore. It was decayed and of no use to me. It had been used by the previous owners to store tools, boxes, paint and many other items. It was filled with cans, bottles, partially empty paint cans and other stuff strewn around. I removed all the cans, bottles and anything that appeared to be hazardous. Then I got my tractor, which has a front loader on it. The tractor made a short job of knocking the building down and placing the whole thing on the burn pile.

I got that job done, and all that was left to do was set the burn pile afire. Before doing that, I pulled a water hose from the yard to the fire, just in case something went wrong, but there wasn't much chance of that. It was just a precaution. I then set it on fire and stood nearby watching the pile as it was being quickly reduced to ashes. The leaves and twigs burned rapidly, leaving only some large limbs blown down during the winter storms, and the large heap of decayed timbers and boards from the old storage building. All was going just fine. I took the rake and went to the pile of decayed boards and timbers and pushed them toward the center of the burning trash pile.

The next few minutes started a totally new and frightening episode in my life. I was standing facing the fire, when suddenly there was a muffled explosion from the burn pile, and simultaneously a ball of fire erupted directly toward me. I recall turning my head and body away from it, but it caught my entire right side. It happened so fast I really did not have time for much body movement or reaction. There was no escape from it. It was too sudden. All I could do was turn away from it. I was wearing a short sleeve shirt and trousers. They were smoking. I did not know at first how serious the burns were.

When that ball of fire hit me, I didn't stand around looking. I ran as fast as I could to the house, grabbed ice from the refrigerator and began using ice and cold water all over. It had taken all of the hair off any exposed portions of the right side of my body, including the hair on my head, eyebrows, and eyelashes. I had burns in my ear and nose. My lips had been hit, as well as my eyelid. On the right side of my face there was a deep burn between the ear and the cheekbone. It was bleeding slightly. My right arm and hand were bright red and hairless. I had gotten rid of the shirt on my run to the house as quickly as possible, because it was hot and I didn't want it to melt onto my skin. The main thrust of the ball of flame was to my upper body.

I stood in the bathroom for probably half an hour using ice and cold water to cool the burned areas. I then called the emergency room at a hospital and told them what had just occurred. I was informed that there was not much they could do except use antibiotics to avoid any possible infection and ease the pain. They would admit me for treatment and observation. They urged me to come in. I declined.

I now gave my face and the other burned areas a good looking at. Those burns were stinging severely now, and I could not only feel the damage, I could see it. I walked through the house, and could smell the stench of burning hair and flesh in every room. I don't know, but I thought it had spread throughout. It took a while for that stench to dissipate, and several people who came over asked me what the stench was. I told them it was me.

I had some huge aloe plants. I had researched them over a period of several years previously and found the juice has some powerful healing properties. I used the juice previously on slight burns and cuts, with very effective results. The American Southwest Indians use it for many purposes, including treatment of major burns and wounds. Aloe is often referred to as the "burn plant." It is also very healing for sunburn. I decided that I would use this for my present problem and began applying generous quantities all over my body on the burned areas.

Everything was healing up real well except for the deep burn between the ear and cheek. It was now scabbed over. Friends who saw it stated there would always be a big burn scar and that I would have to have a skin graft to correct it. I continued to use the juice of the aloe plant many times a day. By the end of the eighth day the scab on my cheek was gone, with only discoloration left behind. I continued the aloe juice treatments for about another week. At the end of that time, there was no indication of my "fireball incident," except for the need to grow back a lot of hair.

Those who saw the initial burns and stated that I would need a skin graft, now said that it probably was not as severe as they had thought. I looked at the trousers and shirt I was wearing that day. They were heavily damaged. Maybe to some this was just an ordinary event with normal healing, but to me, as the victim, it was equivalent to a miracle. I had lived with the burns for eight days, and observed them from start to finish on a daily basis. However, that is only my opinion.

Whatever it was, it worked. I have no scars, and my hair grew back. But this now, in no small way, brought the "voice" to mind. This had been predicted, and the results were exactly as predicted, including the sequence in which they occurred. I had to give this a lot of thought. Still there was no feeling of a "presence" around me. I had had no feeling that it even existed since it made the predictions.

These were only two of the predicted events. There were three. The third one was that I would move to a desert where I would wait until I was given further instructions. My thought was that if the first two events occurred as predicted, maybe there is more to this than a possible illusion. Was the third event going to happen? I had my doubts about that. It just did not seem to be logical. Again, I found myself dwelling on the "presence" and the "voice." I could not help it. I knew one thing for sure: I had no interest or intention of moving to a desert.

Some weeks passed and my life was normal. I noticed that the economy had slowed and was getting real bad where I lived. Then one of the most severe winter storms in many years hit. It was sudden and fierce. It was called a Canadian Express. Temperatures dropped way below zero – an unusual event for this coastal area. Nearly all of the plants on my 31-acre nursery were destroyed or severely damaged.

Over the next two weeks, I assessed the damage and did as much repair as possible. My house was severely damaged also. All of the water pipes froze and broke. They ran through the attic. The pumps to my wells froze and the water lines from them broke.

I was pretty well on my way to repairing all of the damage and was able to move back into my home from the motel where I had to live for those two weeks, when a second storm of about equal intensity hit. It finished what the first failed to do. There was nothing further to devastate. That was when I got the "urge" to move and get out of there. It was pretty depressing to say the least.

I talked to several of my friends about these storms, and inquired if they were going to remain in this area or leave. To the one, they said they were going to stay. It was no problem for them. I told them I was getting the feeling that maybe I should leave this area. They told me it was just depression on my part and that I should forget it and get on with getting things in order.

I listened to them. I knew they were sincere and trying to be helpful. But, that "urging" grew stronger each day. It was really gnawing on me now. I began thinking about places where I would like to move. I kept looking at Houston, Texas; Phoenix, Arizona; and California. I knew some people in Houston and Phoenix pretty well, so maybe I would check with them about the job markets. I knew quite a few people in California.

I began to realize that I really did want to relocate, and each day I wanted to do so more and more. I had lost interest in everything there. I went through the routine of work as a zombie. It was just a mechanical thing. I knew I was going to relocate. I was tied down with a plant nursery and a house. I could not just get up and move. The real estate market was at its bottom, and even worse, it was winter.

While at the nursery shortly thereafter, a man stopped by and asked if he could talk with me. He said he would like to buy the nursery from me. He went on to say that he had been thinking about and looking at it for some time, and as he had a landscaping company and a well drilling company, he felt it would work well for him. We went into the office and discussed his proposition for a while, with the result that we would make a deal. Within a few days, that transaction was complete. In a few more days, a friend of mine called saying he would like to buy my house. I had offers on it before and rejected them, but now it was different. We soon had a deal.

I was free to get out of there. I began making a plan. Nothing really sounded good, so my solution was that I would just leave and go to Houston to see what was there, then if nothing, on to Phoenix. If there was nothing there, then I would go to California. I had no plan beyond that.

CHAPTER 5
RELOCATING

All I had to do now was pack my suitcases and other things that I needed, such as documents, and be gone. That did not take long. I stuffed my vehicle, and was gone. My destination was Houston.

There was a lot of trepidation in me when I left. It was like leaving a part of me behind. That is lonely and kind of a scary thing. I do not know if "scary" is the right word to describe the feelings I had in the pit of my stomach, but I am just going to leave it at that. I knew one thing for sure: I was not going to miss those cold storms or the hurricanes and tornados and the floods generated by them. The last hurricane was just before I got burned in the fire. Much of the debris I was burning was caused by that hurricane and its accompanying tornados. Those are pretty scary things. All one can do is take cover for three or four days and nights and hope the damage is not too severe.

Well, I thought to myself with a little bit of surprise, *now I am doing exactly what the "voice" had told me was going to happen! Did I have any control? Was I completely under its control?*

As I drove along, this consumed my thoughts completely. There was nothing else I could concentrate on. I tried. Can something like this really happen, or is it something out of *The Twilight Zone?* There was no feeling of a "presence" around me. I did not feel my thoughts and actions were being controlled. I didn't have any answers, only questions.

As I neared Birmingham, Alabama, I ran into a major snow storm, an unusual event for that city. The traffic was terrible. There were accidents all over the place, including 18-wheelers going out of control. It took a long time to get through that city, but I made it. I continued my drive toward Houston without incident. As I drove, I thought of many things I had heard about ghosts, spirits, UFOs and alien forms of life. These thoughts of course, were generated by my constant thoughts about the "presence and voice." I figured they must have been one and the same, if they had even existed at all. I thought that maybe they decided to stay in North Carolina and wouldn't be bothering me anymore. I thought that that may be where they existed and couldn't leave. They were not around me now.

I arrived in Houston and stayed there for a few days. I contacted some of the people I knew, and discussed the job situation in that area. It had dried up in the last few years. The oil boom there died. Renting outgoing U-Haul trucks was one of the biggest businesses there now. I thought I would take a drive around the Green Belt that circles Houston. When I was last there, it had been saturated with billboards begging for employees to fill all kinds of jobs. Today, there was not one. The newspapers, which used to have over 100 pages of want ads, now published about one page. I was told that California was the place to go.

I looked around and agreed that this was not the place to be, but not necessarily that the place to go was California. I knew Houston was not it, so I left there for Phoenix. I began watching U-Hauls. It became like a game to me. They were all over the place. I was not meeting oncoming U-Hauls; they were going in the same direction I was. They were the most colorful scenery, though.

One of the subjects that crossed my mind was time. Exactly what is it? It has no weight. It makes no sound – you can't hear it. You can't see it. It surely doesn't take up any space. You can't feel it (until you get past 40). Does it have some form of mass? Does it have motion? Is time a force like gravity or magnetism? Suppose it has some form of mass and motion. According to conventional teachings, for every physical action there is an equal and opposite reaction. Would there then be an opposing reaction to it? What would that be? Would time stop? If time could stand still, then we could walk around in it, possibly. Or, would creation cease, and all we know and see cease to exist?

Some may think these are radical thoughts, but I don't. For example, it takes the Earth exactly 365 days, 5 hours, 48 minutes and 47.8 seconds to make its complete orbit of the sun. These days are based on how long it takes the Earth to make a complete rotation on its axis – 24 hours. There was a problem with the extra 5 hours, 48 minutes and 47.5 seconds left over when the Earth needs a full day to make that complete orbit of the sun. So the astronomers simply put another day into the calendar year every fourth year – leap year. It was in 1582 when it was discovered that there was a 10-day discrepancy in the calendar. This discrepancy was corrected by adding the 10 days to one month that year. Astronomers added the 10 days by making Thursday the Fourth followed by Friday the Fifteenth. This did not interfere with the seven days of the week. The seven-day week is perfect, and has been used since God created Earth.

Everything we do is based on Earth time. I think we pretty well understand that concept because we live it. It governs our lives. It controls when we sleep and when we awaken to go to work at a specific hour and complete our scheduled workday or work-night. We have nighttime and daytime based on the rotation of the Earth on its axis.

But that only works on Earth. On the other planets in our solar system, their rotation on their axes is different from Earth's, as are their orbits around the sun. If we were, say on Jupiter, it would be a much different day and year. Everyone uses Earth time for measurements of time and distance in our entire universe. An entity, say from another solar system, would probably have their own measurement of time, and possibly a different concept, which would probably not even be remotely similar to Earth time. The speed of light may differ depending upon the source of that light, yet we measure all light against that generated by the sun in our solar system.

Is the speed of light consistent throughout the universe? Some time in the past, a human arbitrarily determined the distance a foot would constitute. Using that measurement, they determined what a mile would be. Light travels at about 186,257 miles per second, according to this measurement. Does that same light travel at the same speed throughout the universe? Would the speed of light be different if generated from a sun/star larger or smaller than that light generated by our sun? I do not know, but I do know that what our astronomers and scientists have devised works pretty well for our purposes. Is it accurate? Probably not, but that is only my guess.

I stayed in San Antonio, Texas, that night. The next morning I gassed up and continued west toward Phoenix. The thought of the "voice" was with me again, and I was contemplating just how those predictions were now seemingly becoming reality.

Of course, I reverted to my old standby – just coincidence. This always makes things that one cannot understand or have some rational explanation for easier to live with. If one is not a believer in the possibility of paranormal phenomena, talking with spirits, the existence of spirits or souls, psychic abilities, near-death experiences, life after death, UFOs, extraterrestrial beings, animal spirits, reincarnation or ghosts, then they probably would not have a problem just calling such phenomena the product of one's overactive imagination. I know people who hold that concept, and I know people who used to think that way until one day they had an encounter. I think I was in the non-believer category, but now had graduated to the stage of "possibility."

I had doubts rooted in science and physics, which taught me that such events were strictly imaginary or easily explained away by natural phenomena. On any given Sunday or day of religious observation, you can observe these same scientists and physicists, to name a few, praying to a God they cannot see or touch, hoping their souls go to Heaven. There are ministers, priests, clerics, and rabbis who are not believers, but preach the spiritual existence concept quite convincingly, because it is a pretty good living. (Standing in the pulpit, there may be a culprit.)

Of course, every day we learn of some new "discovery" which contradicts almost everything we have been taught in school and on the job regarding the forces of our universe and solar system — how they work, what they are made of and why they work. I am not contradicting what we teach, only stating that there are many, many, many things we do not know and are unable to comprehend, because we base almost everything we know on what we experience here on Earth.

As I drove along, I really concentrated on the possibility of arriving in Phoenix with myself and my car intact, without having consumed any time. I thought to myself that if there really was a "voice" talking to me, anything was possible with the power of the mind. I concentrated on the odometer and highway simultaneously. The time was shortly after 8:00 a.m. when I began doing this. I do not know exactly how many miles I drove after beginning this concentration, but I think it was less than 10 miles, when I heard a click that seemed to come from the odometer. I was suddenly in some outskirts of what turned out to be a big city. At first I thought I had gotten turned around and was going back into San Antonio, but soon there was a big, obvious sign: WELCOME TO PHOENIX. I was in a lot of traffic.

Looking at my watch, I noticed that it was still just a few minutes after 8:00 o'clock. I thought to myself that there should be nothing ahead for miles but small communities and open road. I looked at the gas gauge, and it still registered full. I thought that maybe there was a suburb of San Antonio named Phoenix and that must be where I was. Soon there was an off-ramp ahead and I could see a service station sign. I got off and parked at the service station, but not at the pumps – I didn't need gas.

I sat there momentarily pondering how and what was going on. I must be mistaken. There has to be a logical explanation. It's a long way between San Antonio and Phoenix. Was I about to wake up from a dream? Many other thoughts raced through my mind in that short period of time I sat there. I got out of the car and went into the food-mart. I got a cup of coffee, and went to the cashier to pay for it. As I did so, I inquired, "Is this Phoenix, Arizona?" That is probably the hardest question I had ever asked anyone. He looked at me in a strange way as though I might be joking and said "yes" in a rather sarcastic tone. I thought maybe he thought I was insulting his store or something there, but I said nothing more, and certainly was not going to try to explain why I had asked that question. As he gave me my change, I glanced at a day calendar by the cash register. It displayed the same day that I left San Antonio.

I knew that I had not just forgotten about a whole day. I did not know what happened, but I had just left San Antonio and at the same time I arrived in Phoenix. No time had elapsed. That is a long distance. I was not even tired. I was not going to say anything about this. There is no explanation. Further, who in the world would buy such a story? It is impossible, and I had never heard of such a thing before. I thought that if that would have happened to someone, they surely would have told someone about it and it would have been known.

I returned to my car and got back onto the freeway. I went a short distance and got off the freeway again and went to a shopping center. I went to a pay phone to call a friend who lived there. I checked his phone number in the phone book to see if it was still the same, and it was. But as I was about to dial, I changed my mind. I was not going to call anyone here. I did not want to be here, live here, or work here. I thought to myself that I would just contact him later. So, I got back in my vehicle and proceeded toward Palm Springs, California. I decided I would visit some friends there and maybe check that job market.

As I drove along, this event was all I could think about until "the voice" came to mind. All of the things it had predicted were happening. If the "voice" was possible, then this is possible. I came up with this question to myself: *Is the "voice" demonstrating to me that there are many things "real" which we humans think are supernatural or impossible, only because we have not experienced them?* I had just had such an experience, and I was skeptical, even more than skeptical – unbelieving – that this had just happened. So I thought that if this could happen once, then it could happen again just as easily.

I attempted to duplicate my thoughts and actions at the time this happened. I thought of being able to travel from Phoenix to Palm Springs without any time lapsing. I concentrated on the odometer. I did this over and over again with absolutely no results. I could not make it happen. There was no audible click from the odometer, only the sound of the engine as I drove every mile of the way. Maybe I wasn't concentrating hard enough. Maybe there was some atmospheric condition that did this.

About a year later, I was talking to a well-educated individual about the "Bermuda Triangle." We were both involved in the aerospace industry and subjects like this came up frequently when discussing electronic failures, electromagnetic pulses and radiation, as well as phenomena which are unexplainable by modern and conventional technology. It was then that he said he had experienced an unnerving event but was reluctant to discuss it with anyone because it was so fantastically unbelievable. He said he previously told his story to one person and had received a lot of ridicule from that person about it. I told him that I would like to hear it anyway and promised that I would not ridicule him.

This is his story.

He was on the East Coast of the U.S. and had to be in Los Angeles in three days. He decided to fly out and purchased his airline ticket. He returned to his hotel room which he had taken for two days. He had not unpacked yet. First, he was going to relax and watch some TV. After watching a show, he got up, picked up his suitcases to place them on his bed to unpack and was standing at a taxi zone at Los Angeles International Airport. His luggage was still in his hands.

He told me that he did not check out of the hotel and still has his unused airline tickets tucked safely away at his home. He said he was walking toward his bed, and then was at the LA Airport, still taking a step with his luggage in hand. He did not know where he was or what happened. He said it scared him to death. He was in a daze. He could not figure out where he was. He thought maybe he had died and was still walking around.

As he looked around, he was able to determine he was at LAX, but was not sure even then. He asked a porter who happened by. The porter told him that he was at LAX and asked if he needed help. He said no, and waited for the next available taxi. He requested the cab driver take him to a nice hotel in the area, which the cabbie did. He spent the next two days sightseeing in the Los Angeles area, and Monday morning he was at his job. He was met by his new boss, and was asked, "How was your flight out?" He replied, "Unbelievable!"

He thinks he was caught up thinking about this job he was to perform and was caught up in some form of vortex, and that, combined with his desires, were transformed into an action. He did not lose those two days. He spent those two days sightseeing. He enjoyed them. I asked him if he had ever been contacted by an alien, or experienced phenomena of any kind. He said he has no recollection of any unusual events and did not believe in this form of phenomena even after it happened to him. I did not relate my experience to him.

I was in Palm Springs by nightfall. It was approximately a 400-mile drive – not bad, just monotonous. I contacted my friend (not the one who I was with when we observed the three UFOs), and was invited to his home. I stayed at his home for a few days looking around at that area's job market. There was nothing available there of interest, even though it is a beautiful and dynamic city.

I went on to Los Angeles. Los Angeles was booming. There were all kinds of jobs advertised in the newspapers. I was having lunch when I decided to call my friend in Phoenix. The answering machine came on, and I left him a message informing him of where I was staying in Hermosa Beach. I was in my room that evening when the phone rang, and it was him. He was on a job in El Segundo with a major defense contractor, and had taken an apartment in Hermosa Beach.

We met and discussed old times, as we had not seen each other in about ten years. His daughter was now 12 and in school, and his wife could not leave her job with another defense contractor in Phoenix, so he had to live here and go home on weekends occasionally. We agreed to share his apartment while I looked for a job. He said he was going to put my name in to his department because there was a position available there.

I was immediately contacted for that job by the department manager and directed to report to personnel for an interview and paperwork. I did that, and completed the volumes of paperwork. Then the wait while my security clearance was being processed. This takes between three and six months. I was required to check in by phone with the manager of the department in which I would be working at a specific time each week to let them know I was still interested and available for the job. If I failed to do this, they would remove me from the list, and I would then be required to wait six months to apply for a new security clearance check. I did not fail to call in.

Now I had a lot of time on my hands. I had had no contact with the "voice" and did not sense that there was a presence around me. I thought maybe it stayed in North Carolina or that I had imagined all of this stuff to begin with, and maybe these were just normal events that I had inflated into phenomena, and the events were just coincidences. These and many more thoughts were going through my mind. I wasn't telling anyone about them, either.

I visited all of the sights that tourists visit when they come to Southern California – some more than once. I had visited some of the sights before, and others I had never seen when I previously lived in California. The amount of change that takes place in an area is amazing. It is in constant change. When one lives there he or she does not notice it because it is so gradual. When you return some time later, you are amazed at all of the changes. That was my case.

I knew some people in Las Vegas, Nevada, who were managers of a time share project there. I decided to drive over there and visit them. The drive to Las Vegas is long and very desolate. The most exciting thing on the way is the 134-foot-tall thermometer at Baker (the gateway to Death Valley) commemorating the Earth's hottest recorded temperature, which was recorded there at 134 degrees.

I went to the time share resort that my friends were running. We visited for a short time and they put me to work there. It was okay, but that wasn't why I went there. I called in weekly to the manager at the defense contractor. That was the job I wanted, and it was now just a matter of time before I could start work there. In a couple of weeks I thanked them for their hospitality and returned to Hermosa Beach.

I wanted to look around in the Antelope Valley, which is located north of Los Angeles, but is still in the county. There are the cities of Lancaster and Palmdale, as well as an Air Force facility – Plant 42. Rockwell, Northrop, and Lockheed have large manufacturing facilities at the plant. The space shuttle manufacturing facility is there. I took a day on a weekend and drove out the freeway to the valley. I looked around, and it was dynamic, I will have to admit, but there was a pretty good dust storm blowing through that area, and it was bad. Even with that, I took my time and looked at as much as I could. Housing and businesses were going up every place. What had previously been open desert was now being filled with housing for workers. I was not especially excited about this area, but there was some intrigue with the industry there.

A couple of weeks later, I decided I wanted to see the area again. The weather forecast indicated only light winds and scattered showers. As I approached a viewpoint overlooking the Antelope Valley, I pulled in to take in the view. I got out of my car and walked over to the rail. It was a beautiful view. You could see building taking place all over. Rockwell was building the B-1 bomber and the space shuttle there. Northrop was building the B-2 bomber there. Lockheed had a huge facility to keep the U-2s maintained and flying. What else was there is top secret. It was a huge facility built around the Palmdale Regional Airport. One could see the huge parking lots at each of these facilities. They were packed with automobiles.

As I stood looking out upon this scene, sipping on a cup of coffee I had carried with me, a rainbow began forming in the distance. It was beautiful and I watched it for a few minutes. Then another rainbow began to form over the other, and now there were two rainbows. I thought this was a beautiful sight. I watched the rainbows as they began fading away when I recalled the "voice" telling me that when I got to the place I was to live, it would give me a sign and I would know the sign. I asked myself, *I wonder if this is the sign.*

No sooner than I had thought that, the "voice" said very distinctly to me, "This is where you will live and work until I contact you again. I had told you I would give you a sign when you arrived at a place in the desert where you would work and live. It was very important that you thought of that conversation with me while noticing the sign. You must listen carefully to what I say. I will let you know when you are to meet me. I will at that time show myself to you. You must be mentally prepared to accept this. You must not be afraid of what lies ahead. No harm shall come to you from this. You must be mentally prepared to do what I tell you to do and have the faith that I am real and this is happening to you. When it is time for us to meet I will cause you to go where the meeting will take place. There will be no further contact with you until that meeting is to take place."

There was no one there – just the "voice" and a charge in the air that felt like static. As soon as the last word was spoken, the static left. Now there was no charge in the air whatsoever. There were a couple of other cars in the scenic view turnout. I looked at them and they seemed unaffected by what I had experience. They seemed to have not seen, felt, or heard anything. As for me, I was disturbed by this encounter, but, as strange as this may sound, I was getting used to it – not the feeling of apprehension when I was contacted, but the contact no longer shocked or surprised me.

I got back into my vehicle and proceeded toward Lancaster. I wanted to look around there to see what kind of housing was available. The defense contractor, Rockwell, was the company I was going to go to work for, and I thought that I might be assigned to this facility. There were a lot of nice homes in this area, and they were reasonable. As I drove around, I wondered what the "voice" meant when it said – It was very important that I think of that conversation while noticing the sign. If I had not noticed the sign would something have happened to me? I do not know the answer to that, but it did concern me.

One morning soon after this, the phone rang. It was my new employer advising me I had met their requirements and had the job. I was now to take a drug test and if successful, I would report to work the next Monday morning. I passed the drug test and did report to work as directed. It was a real good job and I thoroughly enjoyed it. I did not get assigned to work at the Plant 42 facility. I was at the main offices in El Segundo, but I was required to do a lot of traveling. I lived only about five miles from there. But it was a slow, slow drive to work (about 40 minutes) in the mornings and the same back home in the evenings. That would work for a while.

I did not like living with all of the congestion of the Los Angeles area. Besides that, I was only a temporary roommate for my co-worker. I began looking around for a new place to live and decided to go back to the Lancaster area. It took a few weekends to find a rental place that I liked. The most important part was that the area was not congested. It was about an hour drive (75 miles) each way to work and that is not bad; of course, that was not at the 55-mile-an-hour speed limit. The last person who drove those freeways at 55 miles an hour had a long white beard and had been confined to a rocking chair for years before.

I signed the rental agreement and moved into the Lancaster home on the first of the month. It was okay. I enjoyed it. It was not a dull life, but there was nothing exciting except that I had begun building a home. That did not take much of my time. The building contractor did it all. When it was done, I only had to move in.

My life went on like that with absolutely no contact from the "voice." We are not talking days, weeks or months – we are talking years. I had placed the "voice" so far back in my mind that I only rarely thought about it now. When I did think of the "voice" it was to recall that it had said I was to live and work here, and wait for it to contact me. If it did have some type of "deed" for me to do for it, why was it taking so long to tell me what it was? Further, it said that

I was not to grow impatient. Well, I certainly was not impatient for it to contact me again – I did not want it to contact me at all.

It is strange that when these types of things are happening to you they are so real, but as time goes by and the event somewhat fades, you rationalize it more and more as coincidence. Pretty soon, that rationalization of coincidence turns into a feeling that it was impossible and was all your imagination. Those were my inner feelings, but I knew there was a lot more to this than I could ever understand or explain. And deep down inside me, I knew the "voice" would return as it said it would!

The contract I had been working on was now over. The project was completed, and I was now working as an independent contractor, which gave me a great amount of free time. I really liked that, because I could set my own days and hours.

One evening that peaceful and tranquil lifestyle all ended! As I was sitting in my living room watching television that same old feeling of the "presence" came over me. It was all around me. I knew what it was and expected the "voice" to say something. It said nothing, but there was the most powerful "urging" sensation, like a control, that I was to go to Las Vegas the following Saturday. There was no voice. The presence faded away.

The first thought that came into my mind was that this "urging" feeling, was no big deal; people were going to Las Vegas every day from all over the world. What would I go to Las Vegas for? I do not like to gamble, even though I have. I didn't want to visit my friends there right now. But the most important thing was that I really wasn't interested in going back there.

By Friday of that week, I knew I was going to go to Las Vegas. I was not going there to gamble or to see some of the fantastic shows they have at nearly all of the casinos. I knew that I was going to actually meet with the "voice" or "presence" or whatever it was going to call itself. It had told me some time ago that when it was time, it would contact me and tell me where it would meet me. I knew that is what this would be! I could not miss this opportunity. The feeling that this was going to happen was as though I had been told that, but I had not. I cannot now, nor could I then, verbalize it or put it into words. I knew this is what I was supposed to do. I did not, however, know where I was supposed to go when I got to Las Vegas. Was I to just check into a hotel or what? I decided I would just wait and see what would happen. If nothing happened, I would simply enjoy Las Vegas for a couple of days and return home.

Friday arrived, and when I got home from work that evening I called a hotel in Las Vegas and made reservations for two nights just to make sure I had a place to sleep. I grabbed my bags, which I had already packed, and departed. About four hours later I caught the lights of the city and was soon there.

CHAPTER 6
MEETING AN ALIEN

When I arrived at the outskirts of the city, I took the off-ramp to the Strip and fought the traffic to the hotel where I had made the reservations. While checking in at the registration desk, several thoughts passed through my mind. The first was, *What a waste. I received no indication or sign, nor did I have any feeling about where I was to go.* I completed the check-in and went to my room.

I sat there thinking of the lack of communication from the "presence" or "voice." There had been none on my way here, and there was none now. No feeling or urging – nothing. *I am just spending a weekend in Las Vegas,* I thought. *That's all!* I sat there thinking about this for quite some time. The TV had been on all of this time, but I have no inkling what was on. I picked up the key to the room and headed to the elevator for the ride down to the casino floor.

I was beginning to feel some hunger pangs, so I went to a restaurant in the hotel. I ordered my dinner from the house specials. While waiting for dinner I began reviewing the series of events that had brought me here. One of my thoughts which had been a frequent visitor to my mind for some time was, *Why was I doing this based simply on an imperious voice that had no visible substance? Now I am sitting in a restaurant in Las Vegas based on an urging to come here.* That is not natural, nor explainable, in scientific terms. I recalled that in scientific thinking you should be able to test something in order to prove validity. If you cannot test it, then it does not exist. If it is pseudo-science, you cannot test it.

I was in a quandary over this. There was no scientific test that I could apply that would validate the "voice" or the "presence," and there was no test that would prove it did not exist. Is there such a phenomenon as predestination or predetermination? *If there is,* I thought, *then I had no choice in the matter of my presence in Las Vegas at this very moment.* It had already been predetermined. If that is valid, then there is no other man on earth who has a choice as to what happens to him from one moment to the next.

I could not buy that theory. *Man has a free will, and I did not have to be here if I really did not want to be here,* I thought. Possibly the only reason I was there at that moment was merely an overwhelming curiosity to see if something would happen. Everything moved so slowly in this matter that I thought maybe they were further testing my patience. They had told me to be patient.

My dinner arrived and broke up these thoughts. I took my time eating and considered everything. When I finished I walked around the casino for a while and watched the people gambling. They did not seem to be happy like the advertisements indicate they should. I then retired to my room for the night thinking to myself, *If I came here only to have a good time, something was really wrong.*

As I fell asleep, I gave some thought to the "voice." Was it really going to contact me and meet with me? Was it going to meet me here in this room? What was it? What does it look like? Is it dangerous? Was it going to be a monster of some kind that was slimy and ugly? I fell asleep with these thoughts.

I was awakened from a sound sleep by the "voice." I quickly turned on the lamp on the night stand, and looked at the clock – it was 4:30 a.m. There was no one there, but I could feel its presence. It was a powerful presence. It was all around me. The "voice" then said to me, "You will now arise and drive in a northerly direction on a highway. I will direct you as you proceed. You will know which route to take. When you arrive at a certain point, I will tell you. There you will wait for me to appear to you." The "voice" and the feeling of the "presence" left instantly. I had some questions. "Are you still here," I asked. There was no response. It was gone.

I quickly arose, took a fast shower, dressed and went down to the restaurant where I had breakfast. I then went to my vehicle and drove to a convenience store where I gassed up and filled my thermos with hot coffee. I got out the map and looked for the highway that went north. As I was leaving the driveway of the convenience store, I was given directions to that highway going north. *Wow,* I though to myself, *what is going to happen now?*

Finally, I was out of the city and onto the designated highway. The "presence" and the "voice" were with me, and had given me instructions. It wasn't the highway I thought it was going to be. I had never been on that highway nor had I even heard of it. I wondered where it went.

The city was now behind me, and I was driving through countryside that all started to look so much alike I thought I had already been there only moments before. The "voice" had left me as soon as I got onto this highway. I had driven for a long distance and I could feel it was back with me again. It urged me to continue to drive further.

I arrived at a small community called Alamo. The "voice" told me to take a highway at the T-intersection by going left and then to continue driving on that highway until I was contacted again. The landscape was even more barren than before. I knew this was the area where the government and private enterprises carried out extensive secret tests. Nellis Air Force Base has a huge section of this area. Large portions were reserved as a nuclear test site where many underground tests had been conducted. There were other areas – Groom Lake and an area referred to as Area 51. But you could not find Area 51 on any map. There were barbed wire fences alongside the highway with signs that said "do not cross" posted periodically.

The most amazing thing to me was that there was very little traffic out here. I had not met but one vehicle since I had turned left at Alamo. *There couldn't be much out here,* I thought. The scenery consisted of things such as a road off the highway going up a hill or a small structure sitting in the distance way off the highway. It seemed so dead and lifeless there.

Then the "voice" said to me, "You are to turn the vehicle around, and proceed in the direction you just came. There is a turnout in the highway soon after you turn around, and you are to stop there and wait." While the "voice" was giving this direction, I noticed a turnout directly across the highway from me. I slowed and turned around. When I got back to the turnout I pulled in and parked about thirty feet from the highway. I turned the ignition off and sat there. I expected that at that moment the "voice" would show itself to me. I asked myself, *How is it going to do that, and what is it going to look like?* I was anxious, nervous, excited and probably afraid. I could not tell you that for sure, though. I expected it to appear immediately.

It didn't. I sat there for at least thirty minutes and nothing happened. I got out of the vehicle and walked around for a few minutes. Still nothing was happening. I have to tell you this: when I first got there, I did not want to get out of the vehicle. That way, if I didn't like what I saw, I could leave quickly. I got the thermos out and poured a cup of coffee. I had forgotten that I had it with me because of all of the things going on. I leaned against the front of the hood and waited while sipping on the coffee. I could see a vehicle approaching in the distance heading away from the city. It was real quiet out there and I could hear it a long way off. As it approached it got louder.

I contemplated the Dopler sound and waited expectantly for the change in engine pitch as it passed by. The occupants looked my way as they passed and slowed to see what was happening. I nodded to them that I was okay and they kept on their journey, whatever that may have been.

At least another half-hour had passed and still there was nothing happening. I poured another cup of coffee, and began sipping on it. There had been no other traffic. But soon I heard the purr of another vehicle approaching from the north. It was approaching at a real high speed. I wondered if this was whom I was supposed to meet. Was this the entity I was to meet? Was it coming in a fast car? Was it going to stop? My answer came soon enough. It was a Ford Mustang occupied by a man and woman. As they passed, they glanced in my direction and did not slow. The grim looks on their faces made me think that they were on their way to Las Vegas and were practicing the "look" of gamblers expecting to win with the next pull of the slot handle or turn of a card. I watched the vehicle disappear into the distance. I thought to myself, *I guess this "voice" is not going to arrive in a speeding Ford Mustang today.* As a matter of fact, I didn't know how it was going to show up or what it was going to be arriving in, if it arrived at all.

Still nothing was happening. Why did the "voice" give me directions and then make me wait so long? The "voice" was with me as I turned the car around to park here, then it went away. Where was it now? Did it go away, or was it even there in the first place? Why would it do that? I had a lot more questions than answers. As a matter of fact I had only questions, and no answers. I began thinking that maybe this was some kind of government thing. I was keenly aware of all of the secret experiments and testing that were conducted here.

Was I the subject of one of these experiments? I had read accounts in newspapers and magazines about UFOs and strange aircraft seen throughout this area. Does this have something to do with one of those? I thought, *Why though?* I had no answers for that either, just more questions.

There are accounts of UFOs abducting humans, and for some unknown reason performing experiments on them. Was I going to be one of those? I had some concerns about that now because this whole thing was getting more and more strange. But, if so, why me? As newspaper, television and personal accounts of such abductions had been related, in most cases there had been no prior contact with the subject(s), just a quick appearance of a UFO and a sudden abduction without warning or a willingness on the part of the abductees to participate. I really wanted to know what was going to happen to me, if anything at all. I had not been abducted up to this point – just told what was going to be happening. I still felt that I could simply disregard all of this and walk away.

I continued to wait, even though I was seriously considering returning to Vegas. I was feeling a little bit, if not a lot, foolish for being here, because in my mind I was becoming more convinced as each minute passed that this was all in my mind and I had just imagined it; there was nothing to this. It was just in my mind.

As these thoughts were rolling around in my head, I felt a sudden static-like presence in the air around me. It stayed for a few minutes then faded away. I thought that this must have been caused by the fear I was experiencing. But I recalled in the past it had never been like that. There had been some kind of message. But, not this time. There was not a thing. My doubts arose again. *I was here only because of my mindset,* I thought, *not some "presence" directing me.* I looked across the barren landscape. There were no aircraft flying about, no UFOs – nothing.

I walked around slowly sipping the last of the coffee I had brought. More time passed when I noticed there was another vehicle approaching in the distance. Again, the occupants looked in my direction, slowed somewhat, then accelerated and proceeded down the highway and out of sight. At least a passing car was a break in the monotony I was experiencing. I was almost looking forward to the next one.

I finished the coffee and placed the cup back inside my vehicle. I walked back to the to the front of the vehicle and stared off into the desert, wondering if there was really all of that stuff out there that was rumored to be there. I was sure I had been visited by the "presence" while here, but nothing came of it. Why? If I was not going to be visited, why was I here? If the "voice" was real, it should tell me. I had followed what I thought was its instructions and am waiting here exactly in the location where I had been instructed to stop. I contemplated this for a few minutes, and then decided that it was about time for me to get going and get out of there because nothing was going to happen. This was getting to be ridiculous, if it wasn't already.

If the "voice" should want to contact me sometime in the future it could, I thought. I got into my vehicle, and as I was about to turn on the ignition, the air became like static again – only this time with much greater intensity. I had never felt that great an intensity before. It was really strong. I exited the vehicle and put the keys in my pocket, then walked to the front of the vehicle and to the edge of the turn-out bordering the seemingly endless desert. Nothing was there so I walked back to my vehicle. The "static" was still with me, and as I looked around for some visible cause of the static, a "voice" spoke to me.

It said, "Fear not as I become visible to you. There will be no harm come to you." Instantly, before me, an entity became clearly visible. It was not in a mist or vapor. It was not a shadow or some slinky figure, it had its own shadow, just as I had my own shadow. There was not a slow materialization. It was instant.

It was a frightening moment for me, and I felt that this could not be real. It was real, even though I felt I was in an unreal world at that moment. With all of the contacts I had previously had with the "presence" and the "voice," I was absolutely stunned when it did appear. My first impulse was to get away from there, and quickly, but all I could do was stand and stare at what had just appeared before my eyes. It had not materialized from either side or above. It appeared directly in front of me where I had my eyes focused on the source of the "voice."

The entity standing before me was some living thing that I had never seen the likes of before. It had the basic human-type form, but much different from our appearance. I had seen drawings depicting aliens, and this looked kind of like those. It appeared to have many human characteristics, shape and form. It stood looking at me for what seemed an eternity. It said nothing and I could just stare back in fear with an absolute sense of imminent danger. Now I recalled those reports of aliens grabbing people and taking them aboard spacecrafts and subjecting them to various medical/psychological experiments. Afterwards, they were left confused, lost, socially and psychologically unsound. I thought, *Is this the type of experience I am about to encounter?*

The entity spoke. He said, "My name is EM. You will call me by my name when you address me or refer to me from this day forward. You shall use no other name. I bring you no harm, nor shall I bring harm to any other. I am the one who has been in contact with you by voice. The vision you had was that of another of us. This has all been very deliberate, as you have been selected by us to carry out a very important mission, not only for us but for humankind on Earth. It is necessary that you do this. I will help you carry this mission out. You shall not be fearful of me, for there is nothing to fear. I have come to Earth with love."

I stood transfixed while he said this. I wondered if I could speak now. Should I dare say something? Even if conversation was permitted, what in the world would I say to EM? I didn't even know what it was or where it was from. I began to think that maybe it was from one of the nearby military installations or secret areas. Was this some kind of secret government project or experiment? All of this time (probably only seconds but seemed like hours to me), it stood patiently looking at me saying nothing and letting my mind go wild.

I had waited all of this time to meet this entity, and now here it was standing right in from of me. This is the moment I had wanted. Now I knew I was not going wacko – I could see it. How would I explain it?

I was totally, absolutely awe-struck by this entity. Even though I was shaken and confused, I was going to find some answers, or at least ask some questions that were storming through my mind. I had never been given the opportunity to ask either the "presence" or the "voice" anything. Getting up some courage, and speaking for the first time, I asked, "EM, who are you?"

The reply came quickly, with an admonition, "You are not pronouncing my name correctly. It is EHM. Not E-M. My name is spelled EHMR, and is pronounced EHM(the H is real faint and the R is silent). You cannot grasp the significance of this and it is not necessary that you do at this time. When you write my name it shall be capitalized at all times. It is very important that you capitalize my name, for it has significance beyond what you now know. Humans associate each other by names. We do not truly have names, but are known by what we are and what we do – it is similar to a title. I will not tell you what it means at this time."

There was a pause, or so it seemed to me, to let this message be clearly understood by me. I felt that I had been clearly chastised, as though I had been wearing sunglasses during a meeting with the CEO of a large corporation. Then EHMR proceeded, "I am from a universe which is beyond your comprehension and understanding, and beyond that of the best intellectual, scientific and religious minds of humans on Earth. I am not from the planets, stars or galaxies revolving around the center of your universe. You will have many questions and inquiries for which you will be seeking answers from me before this day is done. I will give you the answers to your questions, but only those answers which are necessary, because you could not begin to understand the answer and would become confused."

EHMR stopped talking at that point and poised his head toward me expectantly, as if I had questions. I realized that EHMR had kind of answered my question and at the same time was direct. Still, I wanted to know – Who was EHMR? This was the only question I could think of. It was the most important. I was frozen. I was dumbfounded by this whole thing and could not ask a single question. It seemed like I could not speak. I just stood there.

It seemed like an eternity passed. I had already had quite a few eternities today, and it was still going on. Then EHMR spoke again. "You are full of fear. You should not be fearful. I have a mission for you and to properly perform this mission you must be of clear mind regarding who you are performing this mission for. You must be at peace with yourself to properly perform. You must clear your mind of the confusion you have. I am here to do no harm to you or anyone on Earth. I request you relax and pose your inquiries to me in an orderly manner so you will understand what you are asking and why you are asking it. I will answer any question you have to the best benefit that your understanding and comprehension are capable of."

EHMR was correct. I did not understand thoroughly what had just been said to me. I now wondered if EHMR was a male or a female. This was going to be a tough question to ask, but I was going to ask anyway, even at the risk of being rude. I asked EHMR, "Are you male or female?"

"I am male," he said.

I then asked if there were also females where he was from. He responded that there were. I wanted to know more about this so I asked EHMR what the difference between them was. His answer was that the male is larger than the female, and that both the male and female have reproductive systems; further, this was required so the necessary union between male and female to procreate to produce new life may continue, just like on Earth. But at the same time, it was much different. He went on to say that to create a new soul where he is from, it takes the union of the souls of the male and female.

I was now able to think a little more clearly. He was answering my questions. I wondered just how far I could go with this type of questioning. I asked him, "Are you God"?

He replied, "No. I will explain this to you later. Before we go any further, I must have your answer. You must state whether or not you will perform the mission I have for you. If you agree to perform this mission, you must do so. You have a choice. Either you accept or reject it. It is all up to you. I must have your answer now in order to answer any further questions you may have. If you decline to perform this mission, that is all that needs to be said. It is done, and you shall have no further contact from me. If you commit to perform this mission, then you must do exactly as I direct. What is your answer?"

WOW! I thought. *This is heavy.* Here is this alien standing before me asking me to perform some mission about which I know nothing, and I don't know anything about him except that he is not God, is not from this planet or even this universe. I noticed that when he spoke to me it did not appear he was speaking with words, but with thought – mental telepathy. I could not see his mouth move. I could feel his words, just like I could feel and know what the "voice" was communicating to me. I wondered if he could read my mind. He seemed to know what I was thinking before I said anything. This was confusing.

I turned away from EHMR to ponder my answer. I was so curious and at the same time frightened to find out what this was all about, that I had this overwhelming desire to say yes. I did not want

CHAPTER 7
THE MISSION

I had committed to perform the mission for EHMR. What had I just done? I had many questions for him, and hoped he would answer them. I was also hoping that the mental telepathy that was used as a communication mode was being properly understood by me. Was there a chance I could misunderstand what he meant? I had never had this experience before. He sent telepathic communications to me, but I was unable to get a thought communicated without speaking. He knew what I was thinking, but made me ask each question verbally anyway.

I wanted to know the answer to my next question very much. I asked, "As you stated, you are not God. Is there a God?"

He replied that there is a God, and God is the intelligence that created all of the things in all of the universes, that there is a great plan and the creation of all things is not an accident. He stated that God is more than just a creative force. He is an intelligence that humans, at this time, do not and cannot understand.

With this in mind I asked, "Is there then, more than one God?" EHMR replied, "I will not answer that question for you at this time. As all humans do, they do not use their intelligence properly – they are looking for the easy answer, when in fact, they should be seeking wisdom through their own minds, not from answers by others. I will expand on your question somewhat. God is the creating force of all of the universes. They are orderly, as all things have order. There are those who have been chosen by God to carry out his creative nature."

My next thought was, "Why would EHMR be visiting Earth?" so I asked him that question.

He replied, "I will cover that as we go along, but first you must have knowledge of the origins of man on Earth. As I have explained to you, I am from a universe so distant from your own universe you could not comprehend it. Also, you will have a problem with the fact of the existence of many universes, similar to, but unlike your own. In my universe we do not tolerate evil. Humans originated in my universe. They became evil, or as you may want to call it, defective. Each human has a free will given by God. Humans are the only creatures on Earth who have free will and reason. God created that. Those in my dimension who choose to not exercise social values are deemed to be evil. They have elected that freely. A society or civilization cannot function with evil at its heart. Evil is not natural. All of the universes are of a natural order, as are all things God has created, even Hell.

"Those in our dimension are being culled out at Home, just like you place those who do not conform to your social norm on Earth in prisons. We searched many universes and selected Earth and several other similar planets in your galaxy as the most likely place to transport some of the intrinsically evil. There are six planets, somewhat like Earth, in your universe. There is a tribunal at Home that determined where the social misfits would be placed on Earth or the other planets, in what you may want to call prison colonies. Each planet's prison colonies are similar to those on Earth. Humans, as you call yourselves, were engineered by us to survive in the Earth environment. The body is unimportant. The soul is all that is important. The soul is in the image of God. There is no way these prisoners may ever return to their Home unless they conform to the social standards that befit civilized societies while they are here on Earth. They know when they are evil. It is their problem and choice of destinies, no one else's."

I asked EHMR how they set the prison colonies up. He told me that the prisoners, both men and women, were transported from Home to each planet's individual colonies and that they came without clothing, tools, food, maps or books. If they could not work together and conform to the necessities of survival, they would simply perish. There was no second chance, because they cannot return Home with defective souls. That is why they were ejected in the first place. Your return Home is not a matter for other Earthlings to determine. Only you determine that. You cannot lead a life of evil while on Earth and be reunited to Home. No other human can forgive your sins to God, only each human has that capacity and responsibility. As all things are natural by the natural order of the universe, something that is not conforming becomes nonexistent as far as Home is concerned. The soul must go some other place upon the demise of the body. The demise of the body is simply a natural process. Where will the soul go?

I asked EHMR, "Do all humans have souls?" He said that all humans have souls. He further stated that each of us is missed at Home, and he was here to let us know that they, our relative at our Home in EHMR's dimension, want us to return.

I asked EHMR if dogs, cats, horses, trees, pigs, ducks, fish, worms, spiders and such things have souls. I thought he said that they do not have souls. I was somewhat shocked by this, but if he said that, it must be so. I wanted more clarification on that because I have had pets and animals that I felt close to and they felt close to me. I asked him if I had been mistaken in my interpretation of his communication to me.

He said that I had misunderstood what he said, and then clarified this communication. He said his interest here on Earth was only for human souls. He went on to say that all animals have a soul, but that it is much different than the soul of a human. He said there are others who have the concern for the souls of animals. He told me not to become confused by equating the soul's of humans with the soul's of other living things.

I had been invited to ask any question I wanted, so I did. I asked him what Home was like. He informed me that I could not understand it, but there was no evil, or what we call crime, accepted there. He told me that when a soul is defective, it cannot stay there. If a soul is defective, it cannot return there. The defective souls are sent to one of the planets, such as Earth, for a period of time to rehabilitate themselves. If they cannot do that, they cannot return. "At Home there is still a place higher that we go after death (as you call it on Earth) but we call passing to a higher plane. We are very productive and detest any form of violence. While living, our lives are full of joy, friendship, and happiness. We aid and assist each other. We love our families and relatives, which you here on Earth are a part of. That is why we are here. We want you to return and will help all of those who will listen."

I asked if a man and woman who are married on Earth would be reunited as husband and wife if they should both be worthy to return Home. He said it is not the same way they would be reunited at Home as it is here on Earth. He said it is totally different and humans are unable to understand the concept.

I then asked him if there was such a thing as ghosts or spirits wandering around on Earth. He told me he was not going to answer that at this time, but at some future date he would go into that with me if I should become worthy to know.

He told me that there are higher places to go after we here on Earth have returned Home. That is called Heaven here on Earth, but getting back Home is our first step. Those that are worthy here on Earth go Home, not to Heaven. He said he implores each human to work hard to get back Home. And, it is not easy.

I then asked EHMR this question: If humans were able to build a spacecraft capable of reaching the Home planet in your universe, would they then be Home?

He said, "No. First of all, it is impossible for mankind to build such a craft, because the universe they have been imprisoned in does not contain elements necessary to invent such a concept. Mechanical craft could never reach Home. To reach Home must be through a dimensional and mental concept, not mechanical. With the mental capabilities developed to a full extent, humans would be able to move great distances quickly through space without the assistance of mechanical devices, but they would not be permitted return entry at Home until they had rehabilitated themselves here on Earth."

There was one more thing I wanted to do. That was to reach out and touch EHMR. I asked him, "May I touch you? I would like to know if you are solid matter." He said that I had permission to touch him. So I did. I felt his arm and his chest. He was solid and felt like I would expect a human being to feel. I guess I had expected him to be of the composition of a ghost, because the highway patrolman had driven right by us and had not seen either of us or my vehicle. I did feel better knowing that EHMR consisted of solid matter. I was certain he was not a ghost or illusion.

EHMR then went back to the subject of my promise to do the mission he had for me. He asked me again, "Do you promise to do this mission?"

I said, "Yes, I promise to do the mission you have for me. I already said I would, why do you ask me again?"

He said that he wanted me to say that I would do the mission three times, so I said again that I solemnly promise to perform the mission. He was pleased, and it seemed to me there must be some significance to promising three times. I did not question that though. He did not ask me to sign an agreement. He only wanted the verbal promise three times. That is all there was to it. On Earth a verbal contract isn't worth the paper it's written on.

With the thought that the highway patrolman was unable to see us,

I asked EHMR, "Why did the highway patrolman drive past us without seeing us or my vehicle?" He told me that it was unimportant at this time for me to know that, but that he would explain it in detail later. All I needed to know now was that it was a form of dimensional movement which was quite simple for him to perform. "Further," he stated, "there are things I am going to reveal to you today that you are not permitted to divulge to anyone, unless you receive my prior permission. I am going to take you traveling soon, and you will learn many things about travel. There are two distinct forms of travel – one is forward and the other is back. You will soon learn that travel and dimensional movement are not the same."

My mind was now quite boggled by all of this. It seemed so unreal to me, but there was EHMR standing directly in front of me, and I knew what he was saying. He in turn understood my thoughts clearly, probably a lot more clearly than I understood them. I wondered how someone could move dimensionally and how they could travel. I realized what a tremendous power that could be. Could it be misused? I thought so. Would I have this power?

I asked EHMR if he had made us and my vehicle invisible when the highway patrolman passed us by. He said that was simply a dimension movement, we were not made invisible. We were just in a different dimension.

I then asked, "Why do UFOs appear, and why can't we see them at all times?" He explained to me that there are UFOs which have been purposefully made visible. There are two different types of UFOs but he said he was not going into that until much later. He said he would tell me about that some time in the future when it was time for me to know.

He said that all of these craft do have a purpose for being here but that has no bearing upon the mission he had for me. I then asked EHMR how long it takes him to travel from Home to Earth. He told me that I could not comprehend this, that all I could think about was distances, such as feet or miles. He said I was not intelligent enough to comprehend what distances in space really mean outside of our universe. He told me to try it while standing right in front of him. I attempted this. I first thought of the moon. I thought of a distance of about 243,000 miles. He read my thoughts, and said to me that I was thinking in miles. I did not try further.

I asked EHMR, "If someone drives by at this moment, could they see us?" He said that they could not for we had moved dimensionally and would remain so until this meeting was completed.

EHMR said that we must move this session along rapidly as he had many things to do. He stated that I should present my questions in a more orderly manner so he could dispatch the answers to me in a logical manner that I could comprehend. I was having difficulty thinking of questions to ask, even though I had about a million of them. He then told me that he was going to take me traveling, that I was to remain calm and not be frightened. Further, I would be safe and would return to this very spot shortly.

I was beginning to feel as though I could talk to EHMR as if he was a friend or neighbor. I was beginning to feel comfortable and somewhat more relaxed – but I was still concerned about who he truly was. Was he telling me the truth? I told EHMR that I did not want to go traveling at this time. I wanted to know what my mission was before anything else happened.

EHMR said, "Your mission is to get what we have discussed, and also what we are further going to discuss, delivered to as many humans as possible. The main thrust of this message to humans on Earth is that we are here to give them direction. They have lost sight of what their true goal is. That goal is to be returned to their Home, which is so peaceful and dynamic they are unable to realize what it would be like. This goal also has a selfish goal, for we want you to return to Home. You are needed, and you are all loved as our children.

"When the races of humans were first expelled from their Homes, they had all of the necessary knowledge and skills to make a proper rehabilitation and be authorized to return. They did not do this. They did not use their skills and knowledge, instead they chose to attempt to control and deceive all of those who were with them. Their rehabilitation is under the most severe conditions. They started a controlled concept of murder and intimidation. Those who knew what had to be done to return Home resisted. That led to wars and idiotic bloodshed. Many humans then began a trend of downward development, while others continued their attempt to rehabilitate themselves along with others who had the same desire to return Home.

"These humans had more knowledge and understanding of the world and Home than modern humans do. They understood where they came from and the tremendous task of rehabilitation under severe circumstances that lay ahead. They realized it was their improper exercise of their free will at Home that got them here. As time progressed this understanding became more and more vague and distorted. They were completely aware of the fact they could only return to their Home by changing their ways. Many have tried and failed, while others have been successful.

"Implanted in the mind of humans is the concept of a superior or creation force. This concept is very valid, for there truly is a force. It is far greater than imagined or experienced by humans on Earth. All humans have a desire and drive to return to the Creator. It is now practiced, called and referred to as religion. The awareness in the minds of humans that there is a Creator exists in the subconscious mind. Religious practices are proper, if in fact they would simply understand the origin of humans and what humans must do to return to their Homes. They cannot return at their own desire to do so. They must meet the requirements of the rehabilitation they have been directed to demonstrate."

I challenged EHMR on this statement. I said, "There is a widely accepted and quite well-proven theory that humans have evolved on Earth, that our ancestors are primates, such as monkeys, apes and chimpanzees; that humans came from the trees and gradually evolved into what we are today. We developed a larger brain and an agile thumb. This has given us the advantage over other things today."

EHMR responded to this in an emphatic manner, the first time he had seemed to be urgent, saying, "Humans did not originate on Earth. They have been placed here from the planets in another universe, and to this day are still being sent here. There are many souls awaiting for a man and woman to conceive. Into that conceived child the soul of the next in line from Home is lodged. The body of the child is the host of the soul. The child has no control over what soul it receives. The man and woman merely provide a body for the soul. The child receives only its genetic code from the mother and father, the soul is provided from Home. That soul has no wisdom or knowledge at birth, but does, as all souls do, have an innate instinct of God, and in life will seek God if permitted and trained to do so. It is the responsibility of the man and woman to provide the environment for the child to learn. A good man and woman raising their children properly are blessed. The man and woman who turn on their child and its soul are in serious jeopardy of losing their own souls. Humans' search for a link between themselves and lower forms of life on Earth is futile, for that link does not exist and cannot exist."

He told me that he now wanted me to go with his agenda because it was necessary for me to see and understand. He warned me that he was going to take me to some places other than where we were standing. He said they would each be different, and that I would then begin to understand what he was teaching me. My thought to this comment was that I was unaware that I was being taught anything.

I guess I was though, for I was sure listening to EHMR in an eager manner. He then told me that we would be visiting several sites of original colonies; that these were many generations of descendants of the original prison colonists. I was not to be afraid, for there was nothing to fear. He told me I would be traveling back in time! I had some real difficulty comprehending this, even if I did at all.

I asked, "Will this affect me in any way? Will I become younger, or what?" He told me my fears were unfounded; there was nothing to fear. We were just going to travel around and see some of the colonies. He told me they would not see us, and that I would not be affected in any way. He then said that I was mentally prepared to go with him, and reached his hand out and touched my left shoulder very gently. "We are now departing this location," he said. I felt a strange rushing sensation throughout my entire body. It was a sudden and anxious moment. It seemed like it was instant, but yet I was completely aware of the feeling of acceleration. It was not a physical feeling—it was a mental feeling. There was no gravitational pull, such as you get against the back of the seat when you take off in an airplane. This was sudden and momentary.

I was now standing beside EHMR on a hill overlooking a lush, fertile valley. There was a river running through it with trees in great abundance growing on each side and fields stretching beyond the trees from one end of the valley to the other on each side of the river. There were groups of humans working in the fields and, not many, but some animals scattered about near the humans. We did not walk down to the valley; we were just there, close to the people and the fields and trees.

I noticed when we first arrived in the valley that there appeared to be villages located at almost specific distances apart, stretching from one end of the valley to the other. They were each surrounded by a barricade of limbs and grasses. They had gates for entrance and exit. Some of the villages appeared to be quite large and others smaller and of varying sizes. Each village had a structure in the center which was much taller than the surrounding hut-like structures. After arriving down into the fields and people, I estimated that there must be about a thousand people in the larger villages that we were in. There were men, women and children of all ages.

While we were moving through the laboring humans, I noticed that they did not look like me all that much, as I had expected. They had a look about them that resembled the characteristics of EHMR, but heavier and courser. They were of a dark-skinned nature which was possibly due to being exposed to the sun and the elements. They had slender builds and faces. Their bodies were quite muscular. Clothing was scant, with most wearing animal skins covering their loins – both men and women. Children wore no clothing. Facial expressions reflected desperation, not boredom, to get the work complete – possibly meaning their survival. I don't know. They were all working hard.

We then went instantly to the area along the river. There were people in the water and on the riverbanks with what appeared to be fishing nets and spears. They were very intent on their task. Trees lined the riverbank. They were of a subtropical nature. They bore fruit that looked like many of the tropical fruits that we have today. I asked EHMR, "Are the trees and bushes bearing fruit that we see here native to the Earth?" He said that some of them were and some had been brought from the home planets for the humans in the prison colonies to ensure their survival. I asked him about the crops in the field. He said that it was equally true of those plants also, and that it was true of the tubers they harvest.

I asked if I could visit the nearby village that was obviously the home of the people we were near. In an instant we were standing at one of the gates to this village. There were mostly women and children here. Most of the women were in the village – only a few were in the fields and at the river. There were many who appeared to be in various stages of pregnancy and all were attending children or performing what appeared to be domestic chores. They were busy and intent. The men appeared to be about twice the size of the females.

The village had a large, tall structure in its center. It was open on all sides. There was a large cone-shaped dome located in the center of that structure – nothing else. There were four women sitting on the dirt floor around it – evenly spaced apart – with theirs arms pointing upward, heads bowed, saying nothing, at least that I could hear. All of the people appeared clean.

It seemed as though we had been at this location for an hour or more. I asked EHMR where we were. He said that he was not going to give me that information, as it was unimportant to me now. I had never seen anything like this before, not in documentaries, geography or history books. I have no true idea where I was but felt that I was in India. I asked EHMR how many people were in this valley. He said that now there were about 250 thousand here and in the surrounding area. He said these people descended from the original prison colony, and had been placed here to survive as best they could, devoid of the advantages of their Home planet civilization, which took eons to perfect. He said they had all been left here to survive using whatever is available to them. He went on to say that they must not only survive, but must rehabilitate themselves as well while here on Earth and exposed to the natural dangers of this environment. They are also exposed to the dangers of those among them who are greedy and power-hungry. This last is the most dangerous to their spiritual well-being. "All of the souls of these people you see, and all of souls of the children you see, were sent here from Home because of their inability to conform to the social standards required."

I had a concern and asked what I thought was a simple question: "Isn't it rather barbaric and cruel to isolate a group of people and all of their children and future generations far from home and in an environment that almost certainly denies them the ability to ever return Home again?"

He stated that this was not an act of barbarism nor was it an act of cruelty. It was simply a means to keep evil from the Home from which they had been transported. These, each and every soul, were the evil souls at Home. They could not remain there under any circumstances as such.

He went on to mention that in recent times humans determined to rid the general populations in England of the evil elements. They shipped them to Australia, where they were left to their own devices to survive, with very slim chances of every returning to England. France transported by ship their most evil citizens to a prison on a small tropical island where they could not escape, nor could they survive. It was a death sentence. The American Indians were placed on reservations located in isolated areas with little food available, and many perished because of lack of proper nutrition. They were generally thought of as undesirable residents.

He asked me, "Did the transport of humans from England, France and America solve the evil in those lands?" He then answered this question himself – "No. Evil still exists in all of these lands. How humans handle that on Earth is their problem, not that of us from Home – that is your problem to solve. We have solved our problem. You are here on Earth, and if you cannot rehabilitate yourself you simply cannot return Home. It is not cruel. We have given you a second opportunity."

He told me that I was just like all other souls on Earth inhabiting a human form. I must rehabilitate myself to return Home. He asked me, "How are you going to do that?" I thought about that for a moment. I want you to know this – I really did not like that. He was talking about me now. I thought that maybe this is why he brought me here – so I would better understand what the mission I am supposed to accomplish really is.

I changed the subject and asked him, "When you speak to me, I do not feel that you are talking. Your mouth does not move. Yet, I understand everything just as though you had said it like I would have spoken it – could you tell me if I am correct?" He replied that he knew my language, but did not speak as I did because he communicated directly with my mind, as he would and does with any human anywhere on Earth. This is not through a language but with a thought impression which is communicated directly to the mind of the human or humans he is directing it to.

He said that if I thought of the work "milk," he would know what I thought, because in my mind I simply have an impression of what milk is, and milk spoken in any language would have the impression of what milk is. He went on to say that if I said the word milk, he would know what I thought, and would not have to hear me. If there were two people thinking of the word milk, each in a different language at the same time, he would know what each of them thought.

I was ready to leave here so I posed a mental thought to EHMR: May we now go to one of the other places you said we were going to visit? I had difficulty posing this question and merely transmitting it mentally; I wanted to also say it. I feel that I did, in my mind, say the words, one at a time. I know that is what I did. However, he had no problem knowing exactly what I asked him. He said we would go soon to the next location, but first he wanted to tell me something, and I must listen carefully to him.

He told me that I must not feel inferior to him just because he knows what I am thinking but I do not know what his thoughts are unless he transmits them to me. He said that mankind, over many generations of being imprisoned on Earth, has almost completely lost this ability of pure thought. Humans have become mentally lazy, and are reluctant to take the time necessary to restore this ability. It takes a lot of consistent effort to accomplish this in even a small way. Those who would take the time to control their thoughts and develop even a small ability of pure thought would find comfort greater than they can presently imagine, which would include abilities far beyond that of the mechanical-practical environment of Earth. Humans use only a small part of their brain, but if they would simply apply their abilities and mental capacities they would be equal to the others of his dimension.

Humans have become dependent, through their mental laziness, on others and mechanical devices to do their thinking for them. Even the people who do their thinking for them rely on a mechanical device to tell them what to tell others and how to tell it to them.

The present-day thrust of human thinking is to rely on electrical or mechanical devices. It is becoming ever more predominant among humans to look toward and rely upon governments, banks, religious organizations and politicians to direct and control our thinking as those groups want you to think and act. That works and is working right now throughout the Earth. This makes it easy for the individual to overlook his own search for the truth, and how his conscience responds to his own thinking, because he doesn't have to think – its all done for him.

These groups, individuals and governments should be serving the people, not enslaving them. There is little care or concern for the greater mass of people. In many cases greed, power, luxury living, deceit and deception, along with false promises of a better life for the masses, will put the people to sleep waiting for the bottomless promises to materialize. People, knowing no better, take the word of governments and politicians that they are doing the will of those people. Most people are looking for a heavenly existence on Earth. They have accepted the premise that greater comfort is of more importance than personal responsibility. Responsibility can be purchased with the promise of comfort.

Look at the former USSR, under Communist rule for 80 years. They were ruled with promises of comfort and luxury if they followed the dictates of the rulers. If they did not follow these dictates, they were killed, enslaved, imprisoned, starved, denied adequate housing and clothing. Education was controlled to the interests of the rulers, religion and a faith in God were denied them – it could go on an on, but the masses never experienced that utopian promise. Instead, while they suffered, the rulers lived in luxury the peasants could not imagine. After the fall of that evil empire, many of the people yearn to have it back, because the government took care of them. They did not have to think.

You must now understand that when EHMR and I left the Nevada site where I met him that day, we did not depart in a spaceship or UFO. We simply departed and reappeared in a beautiful river valley someplace else. It certainly was not anywhere near where we were only moments before. I could not then, as I cannot now, explain in any way, shape, or form how that event occurred. I do know that I was not abducted against my will, because I was there voluntarily and went voluntarily. We were just so suddenly on that hill overlooking that river valley. It boggles my mind. I wondered, *Could humans do that time travel without the aide of an extraterrestrial being?*

With that in mind, I asked if he would take me to the future. He responded by stating that humans do not understand the relationship of time, future, present or past. He said the past and future are one and the same with the present. Time is not understood by humans. He said that humans cannot comprehend what they refer to as space truly is. They are presently seeking to find and explain the center of our universe. They do not know what it is or how it occurred. This universe is not the only universe in existence. There are many millions of other universes stretching endlessly through space. There is no end. Space does not end – nor does creation of universes end.

Humans have no comprehension of that. Everything in this universe is important, each grain of sand and drop of water. But, most important and above all is the human soul. The future is what lies instantly ahead of you. Your future is what is happening right now. Your past is what is happening at that same instant. The past, present and future are one and the same.

Time is something humans do not understand. No one on Earth understands the time concept. I am telling you about the spiritual and dimensional reality now, not the mundane clinical existence of the human body. No human could ever imagine the real vastness of space – there is no end to space or to creation – no matter how far or fast you move within it.

EHMR said he was now going to take me to another part of the Earth where another one of the original prison colonies had been established. We were suddenly in another lush valley where a wide river flowed gently through it. The vegetation appeared to be similar. There were people working in the fields, and the nearby village appeared to have been established in a similar manner to the first colony. Females and children, who were dark-skinned, were tending sheep and goats. I was shown nothing further in that area, and he said very little about the people and their culture.

EHMR said we were now going to visit another original colony site and that he had told me what was most important already. As we left here I was taken somewhere that was just a vast barren land. I could only see its vastness. There was nothing there. I do not know why he showed me this, and he did not expound on it.

He then took me to a third prison colony. We stood in a forest. I asked EHMR where we were, and was told that this was part of what is now Europe. We walked a short distance before coming to a meadow. There was a village centrally located in this meadow. Men, women, and children were all about it. It was a small village. They did not have houses; instead they had what looked like shelters made of branches and skins. They were of very light skin coloration and both sexes appeared larger than the people in the previous two colonies I witnessed before. They had fires, and were obviously cooking food over them. They also had utensils. I did not see much of these people. I wanted to, though. EHMR told me that what I observed were humans shortly after their placement upon Earth. He further stated there was no joy or happiness in them.

We returned instantly to the Nevada site where I had met EHMR. I felt as though I had never left, and that no time had elapsed at all, even though it seemed were visiting the prison colonies for a long time while there. We traveled, we walked, I was shown much, but it now seemed like only seconds. I wondered how many Earth days it would take to go to each of those places from where I was now standing and return to that same spot.

At that moment, I became acutely aware that if I should ever mention what I had just experienced, I would be in for some very serious ridicule from many sources. But, if I should even mention any of the things that were happening to me, I would be in the same spot. So if I was going to discuss one event, why not the whole thing? Besides that, I had agreed to a mission that I was not completely sure was a good idea, and probably would somehow have to divulge everything in order to even begin.

The other problem I was having was the difficulty realizing this could be happening right now. I witnessed things that I could not even imagine what magnitude or significance they bore. I do not believe any human can imagine this. I have been in earthquakes, war, hurricanes, witnessed close-up detonations of an H-bomb and an A-bomb. None of these would even register on the scale with this present event.

I asked EHMR how he was able to travel and take me with him. He told me that, first of all, for some time he had been preparing me to travel. When he placed his hand on my shoulder, he said, that was merely to give me confidence. He stated that if I had no trust or confidence in him, nothing would have happened. He stated he only led the way. That is the power of the mind. At that moment that power was in my mind. He said it is all in the control and development of the powers of the mind. Man must learn to reach into the inner mind and develop that ability. It is there within easy reach, but can be far away if one is afraid of it or too lazy to work hard and take the time to develop that ability. The ability to concentrate on pure thought is the absolute key.

I asked him, "Did you take me to the future or some other planet"? He said no.

As we talked I heard the engine noise of another vehicle approaching and looked to see what it was. Neither EHMR nor I said a word while the car approached. I wondered if they would be able to see us. It began to slow down and I thought to myself that it had seen us and was going to stop. It turned into the turn-out in which we were standing and stopped about ten feet from my vehicle. The occupants, a young male and female, exited the vehicle hurriedly and the female squatted behind the passenger side open door while the male went to the rear of the vehicle. They both urinated. They both looked around and their gazes scanned where we were standing. Neither of them indicated they had seen us or my vehicle. I felt like saying something to warn them that they were not alone but didn't. I was sure she could not see us or my vehicle. I could hear them and wondered if they could have heard me if I had spoken or moved my feet in the dirt and rock. The young man said to her that this was a great relief. She responded with a comment that it was a good thing they stopped and that she was not going to drink anymore beer until they got to Vegas. The young man said they had to hurry because they still had to get their marriage license and be at the chapel for their wedding ceremony scheduled at 6 o'clock.

When this couple departed without even noticing that they were in the presence of two people standing nearby, in broad daylight, and a vehicle parked within 10 feet of them, I asked EHMR why they had not been aware we were right there. He said they could not see us. I asked why then could I see and hear them clearly? He told me that this was something he was not going to explain to me at this time, because it was not time for me to know this. I would not at this time understand it. He said I could not do that at this time, but that sometime in the future I would be able to do so if I was mentally prepared to follow the direction he would give. I thought to myself that he must think I am a pretty dumb human. He picked up my thoughts instantly, and said, "I do not think you are dumb. You need to develop your mind."

With that statement in mind, I became extremely curious as to whether or not I was truly the subject of some government project being conducted at some of the nearby secret installations. Could they possibly have developed a human control system of this magnitude?

I asked EHMR, "Are you involved in, or an agent of any of the government or private sector research projects being conducted in this area we are now in?" He told me that he was not involved with any of them but was totally aware of what they were.

I asked, "Why, then, did you select this location in such close proximity to these government installations for this meeting, with the fence with DANGER and WARNING signs posted on it within a few feet of where we stand?" I was sure I was onto something here, because I know the government has eyes and ears covering every inch of that huge area. If a person should cross that first fence armed security forces will come and arrest you and confiscate any cameras or other electronic devices you may have in your possession, then charge you with trespassing on a top-secret government installation. They also have black hawk helicopters ready to intercept any intruder. If you should cross the second fence, you will be shot on sight. And, they will get you.

He answered my question. He said that he had spent much time here watching the tests and experiments being conducted. He went on to say that he and his companions have also spent much time observing other areas. He said there are other areas all over the Earth where there are people doing similar tests and experiments. Some of that research, tests, and experiments were used to develop weapons that could destroy all of the humans on Earth in the blink of an eye.

He went on to say that they were also observing many research and tests centers that were operating to further human emotional and social well-being, but those were going to be long and laborious projects, because humans on Earth are now basically lazy and evil by nature, and are difficult to rehabilitate or change. He said that this type research should be placed with the highest priority, but it is not. The weapons of mass destruction have the highest priority and the greatest financial support. Weapons mean power, wealth, and control for a few – poverty for many. They consume all of the wealth and resources and have no end value. It is a lack of proper perspective by those with power who are promoting their self-serving special interests in some of the projects. Scientists and other experts will do the work if paid enough money.

"I am now going to conclude our meeting with the final instructions to you for your mission," he said. "As I stated to you before, you shall disseminate the message I am giving you to as many humans as possible. How you decide to do this is entirely your responsibility. This conforms precisely to the agreement and promises exchanged between us. I am now telling you that you shall meet the sixteen who will know what you are doing. There are many who know of this. The sixteen will know you and you will know them.

"Only the sixteen shall be chosen to assist you in carrying out this task. If this task succeeds, many souls will be saved. If it should fail, many will still be saved, and many shall be lost. It is up to you and the sixteen to give direction to others. You are to direct the sixteen who will be selected. They will come to you. There will be many more who come to you. Each and every one of them is of great importance and purpose to Home. Do not turn them away, even the frauds and those who will despise you. No one soul is better than any other soul. They are equal at conception."

He then went on with a warning about what was about to happen to me. He stated that I would be ridiculed by many, believed by some, not believed by some and would undergo many personal trials and hardships. There would be obstacles placed in my path that would seem insurmountable, but I must face those and not lose faith. Furthermore, there were forces that did not want this mission to be done, and I will face their wrath. He told me not to worry about any of that.

He said, "I and my companions will be there to assist you when you need it. We will ensure that you get this message dispersed to as many humans as possible. We will give you special insights and other abilities while performing this mission, but only as you progress on your promise. Do not fear anyone or anything while performing this mission for I will be near at all times. Persist in your mission. You have given your promise and I am giving mine that we will help you accomplish that end."

I asked, "To ensure that I am capable of performing this task, can you, with the obvious powers you have, provide me with some special power now?"

He replied, "You must perform your task as you promised. You must not ask this for we make all such decisions to grant certain necessary abilities as you progress in your mission. We will always be with you when you need us. It is important to us that you do this."

CHAPTER 8
THE SPACESHIP

I had heard clearly what he had said. My concern now was I had a mammoth task ahead of me. The way I understood what he had said is there were sixteen humans out there I had to locate. There are over six billion people in the world. This seemed to me to be an insurmountable task, and I wasn't even sure how to start. Could it be done? I had no idea. I wondered what the odds would be of finding one person. EHMR had referred to "the sixteen," which to me meant that there were only sixteen special people out there I was to find. He had left me to do this on my own with no hints or offer of assistance from him or his companions—only that they would always be near.

I asked, "I know we have discussed this, but I have to ask for more direction and get more information from you on how I am to locate sixteen people in such a massive population. You must have some suggestions. Will you share those with me?"

He replied, "You will know them when you talk with them. You must do what I say, and they will come to you. You can make your contact in any way that you feel comfortable, but you must resolve that problem. They will also know you. There will be many who come to you, trust that I have said that. There will be those that I have contacted before. I have offered them the same mission you have agreed to perform. They refused to accept it, or denied the reality of my contact. You must make the selection of the sixteen. You can freely accept twenty or twenty thousand for this mission, but you shall have no less than sixteen. There will be many who come to you. Do not turn them away! Each of them is very important. They are all important, for they are from my world. You must concentrate on and understand clearly the sixteen.

"You will find frauds and those who despise you. You shall not turn them away, but you will know them. This is your promise and this is your mission. We expect you to do this as you promised, and we will help you when you need help, but only when you need help. You will encounter those who do not believe or do not want to believe that they have been contacted by us for this or other purposes. None of them have responded to perform this mission now assigned to you. Some of those contacted denied from the outset that they had been contacted, but others admitted the contact but refused to perform this mission for fear of the obvious public disdain forthcoming."

He went on to say that those he had contacted were from all walks of life. There were those who had high positions of power, wealth, and politics; those who were poor; those who were greedy; those who were rich and famous the world over; people from all cultures and races and religions; those who were just wealthy and those who were simply average humans. Most all of them denied this contact. Each had a different reason based upon their perception of what would happen to them if they should attempt to pursue the mission or confide in others regarding their experience. There had been those who admitted they have had extraterrestrial experiences, visitations from spirits, contact with the spirit world, contact with UFOs and those with valid "beyond life" experiences, but were all fearful that they would be forever looked upon with jesting by their neighbors and associates. So, they simply kept their mouths shut to avoid ridicule and suspicion.

He said they have been in contact with humans who had and have accepted their mission who became powerful, wealthy and progressive by spreading the messages and disciplines given them. They keep hidden the secrets of the powers given them, because the average human cannot or does not want to understand the meaning of what the messages are. Humans must develop their minds and understand the disciplines by undergoing a rigorous examination before they can be an active part of the mission that I had accepted. This has been going on for centuries in Earth time, and is going on to this day.

He then shocked me with this statement. All humans have a number. All humans from all time have had a number. This also includes not only my universe as well as all of the other civilizations in your universe. Each and every human has a number and each number is significant and is recorded. Lower forms of life do not have numbers, because their souls are not like our souls. Even though they do have souls, EHMR was interested only in the human soul. Each number is assigned to be permanent for all time, and is never repeated. Your number can be canceled, and if it is, will never be repeated. The only way a number can be canceled is if a human does not conform and refuses rehabilitation. Then that number is canceled and a new and far different number from another world is assigned. That number is also permanent and is never repeated.

I had heard that each person had a number. I had heard of the mark of the beast, and that Satan had a number, reputed to be 666. It seemed to me that there would be a lot of digits in each number if each of us had our own special number. Numbers are a vague concept, but the way we use them in everything we do here on Earth works pretty good. We number and name the galaxies in our universe. We number, name, and add other symbols to identify other bodies floating through our galaxy. There are tens of billions of galaxies such as ours (the Milky Way) in our universe. We do not know what lies beyond the center or even where the center is. We are still trying to find it.

I asked if there was a real Satan, or devil? EHMR replied that there absolutely was, and there are many helpers. He then went on saying that there was only one main God, but there were many lesser gods.

He said that the world of Satan is a dimensional domain separate and distinct from that of God. Satan's domain exists simultaneously and parallel dimensionally with the domain of God. Satan's domain is of a nature unimaginable by humans. Evil is Satan's domain exclusively. There is a destiny for evil, and that destiny has many names. Those who should seek evil and death will receive it promptly. Evil has a different number system than all other numbers. Those numbers are totally different and are easily recognized. The absence of good and light are synonymous with evil. Evil has its own energy, and that energy reflects one's number.

EHMR told me he was going to divulge my number to me, and then did so. He told me to tell no one my number. I asked if this number could ever be taken from me. He said that my number could be canceled, and if it should be canceled I would be given a new number for Satan's domain. Other than that, I would always have that number, just like all others have their number. All humans have, and must have, a number. He said that he had disclosed numbers to a few humans before, but the results were not favorable. Some felt that this gave them a right to royalty. Others became so fearful after learning what their number was that they had many problems and would not complete their missions. They all had free will.

I asked EHMR if he had a number. He said that he did, and that his number was from God, like so many others like him on Earth! He said that no person should divulge their number to anyone if they should learn what it is. He told me that he knows the number of all humans because it is stamped on them. He could see my number but no other person on Earth could see it, nor could I. I asked him why did we have to have numbers? He said this should be of little concern to me at this time. He would tell me sometime, but only when I was ready and needed to know.

EHMR told me the sixteen I was to locate could be more than

sixteen. Some of these people would have a feeling that they had been contacted by EHMR's companions for a mission, while others would definitely know they had been contacted. They would also have some concept of EHMR. He said there would be those attempting to be recognized because they feel they have much to offer in the mission, and that would be quite acceptable for they feel they have been called upon to do this mission with me. He said I should help them develop their minds and understand the disciplines.

I told EHMR that there were many questions I still wanted to ask, and I would like to know the answers to them before he left me on my own. He encouraged me to do so quickly because the meeting was about to end. He also advised me, "When I leave you here this day, I will not make visible contact with you until you have your mission well underway. As long as you are progressing on this mission, I will permit you to do so at your own control, but if you should discontinue your efforts, I will be in contact with you. Do not underestimate my resolve in requiring you to complete this mission to the best of your abilities. I now warn you that while you are performing this mission, you will encounter and endure many hardships and frustrations. I tell you now that you shall overcome them. Do not become faint of heart or resolve. We will help you whenever you need it." As I listened to this, I felt about as big as a grain of sand in his presence. I was bigger than him physically, yet he made me feel small. I felt as though I had a heavy weight hanging from my neck.

I asked, "I am now to tell as many humans as possible that they are to rehabilitate themselves, but how do I explain rehabilitation to them when all of the teachings about God and how his Commandments direct us to live a sin-free life are ambiguous?"

He replied, "There is no religion practiced on Earth today that is right or correct. Each of the established religions has taken, and teach, some excerpts from God's law which are correct, but they have changed and ignored those teachings they do not feel suit the selfish purposes and monetary ends they desire. Many in the clergy and other walks of life are driven by materialistic criminal greed and lascivious acts to suit only there own purposes. Many have no concern for the true well-being of the souls of humans who will listen to them. The people have become used to being manipulated and misled. They have become lazy and rely upon some religious leader to direct how they think, when they think, and what they think. Each person knows inside his own mind what is right and what is not right, but it has become easy to permit some other humans to tell you what is right or wrong. That is pure spiritual laziness."

He said that there are some acts that humans perform each day that are neither right nor wrong. These are those things that happen in the daily life of each human. For example, you are walking down a street and encounter a beggar – should you give some money or should you just pass that beggar by? At that moment you must make a conscious decision. In your heart you will have a feeling whether or not that beggar is truly needy or a lazy fraud. Whatever course of action you take is not a sin. However, there is a blessing for you for your compassion toward a fellow human. You will feel this in your heart.

Humans who enthusiastically pursue life on Earth with an understanding of God while keeping the true values of the human souls they encounter and serve as the centerpiece of their own existence, are truly blessed by God. Each human has the responsibility to be productive and useful in their countries and communities regardless of race or beliefs.

No one can be enslaved against their will. Voluntary slavery and slavery within one's mind are not against the will of humans. Excessive and abusive taxation are one form of slavery and are evil. It is used to control the thinking and development of the minds of humans. It controls freedom of movement when excessive and abusive. However, it is the product of people who permit it to become abusive. But when taxation is properly administered for the good of all, it is necessary and productive. I thought to myself at that moment that I did not want to get tangled in that kind of thinking. EHMR read my thoughts, and told me that I would tell this to people because it is important.

I asked my next question which I know is of concern to many now and has been in the past: "Do you, or your companions, want to invade and take over the Earth?" EHMR seemed to be looking into my mind as I said this. He responded, "If we wanted to take over Earth, we could have done so long ago. There is nothing here we want. We could take over Earth in seconds. Do not forget why you were imprisoned here. We would like all of you to return Home after you live your life here on Earth, but you must rehabilitate yourselves while here. We are not sending for you. When you conform you will be returned to your Home. All humans must know that. There is nothing here on Earth we want except that. And that is the only reason for your presence and existence here."

I said that at the rate humans are progressing in engineering, physics, chemistry, mathematics and science, we would soon be capable of traveling great distances at great speeds in space. I asked if it is possible humans could travel to his universe without his help and be Home?

He replied that mechanical devices alone could never get us even out of our Milky Way. We could never escape the universe we are in because we do not have the mental development or the ability to live long enough. We were designed by them to live in the Earth environment and we cannot change that. Home is a different dimension. He went on to state that there are research projects going on at many locations on Earth that are refining space travel techniques dramatically from an Earth point of view, but they rely on mechanical devices.

He said the human mind must be expanded greatly to even begin to understand the expanse of what we call space. We do not even understand the concept of time. Distances are so great that some of the celestial bodies you will be able to observe on the other side of this universe with new observation technology have been gone before Earth was formed. The only thing you will find is the energy emissions still arriving on Earth, but that body no longer exists. All things in our universe are circular. Time has no beginning nor does it have an end. Space has no beginning, and like time, has no end. Humans cannot understand or explain this. Humans do not know when, where, or how the first smallest speck of matter was created. Space is completely filled with matter that we cannot see or understand. Humans can only see a very small part of the total matter in the universe.

I asked EHMR if the matter humans cannot see is affected by gravity. He told me that all things are affected by gravity, but we can only understand how gravity affects us here on Earth and the tiny amounts of space we are able to traverse . There is more than one form of gravity. Humans only observe one form. There are also forms of anti-gravity. Humans must understand those forms before they will be capable of effectively traversing great distances. Humans must understand dimensions beyond the three they observe in Earth's environment. This understanding takes place in the mind, which means that Humans must develop their minds, and use them, far beyond what they are doing. He told me that I did not and could not understand what he was telling me. He stated that he was not going into those matters further at this time.

I had to ask this question, and now I did: "Did you travel to Earth in a space ship?"

He said that they did do so, but that I would not understand what it was. He said they also had come here with other space ships, and that each had many aboard. He said they carry along smaller craft for observation purposes only. The larger ships are base stations where all control is centered.

I asked if we had been on a spaceship when we went traveling. He said, no, we were not, that it was a simple matter to travel here on Earth. He said that was only a step away, but would not elaborate.

He said that life on Earth is a lonely journey for humans, that life is a mystery to them. But it wasn't always that way. In certain civilizations several millenniums ago the secrets of life and knowledge were well understood by many humans who worked hard to develop their minds. They had knowledge and understanding of gravity and anti-gravity, mathematics, astronomy, geometry, and history, as well as many other secrets of the purpose of why they were placed here. They were given that knowledge and discipline by entities such as EHMR and others.

Then for some unknown reason, the leaders determined that no other person but themselves should be entitled to possess these secrets. The purpose of why humans were placed on Earth began to take on a tone of mystery and superstition at the direction of those leaders. There was great power in that knowledge. It was closely guarded by them, and those who were privy to these secrets were sought out for extermination. But, they did not exterminate all of those who knew the secrets. Some escaped and kept the secrets alive by word of mouth and later wrote them down. Even today those writings exist and are hidden in closely guarded secret vaults by the ancestors and heirs of those men who escaped extermination. The teachings of these secrets are done from trusted person to trusted person. The writings are not disseminated. They are in the brains of those who are taught.

When those leaders died they left a legacy of ignorance and superstition behind. The leaders who followed now relied on superstition and ignorance to control the great majority of the masses. It was then that humans lost the true knowledge and understanding of the purpose of life and why we have a body.

There are forces today attempting to locate those written secrets, and the guardians of those secrets are very aware or this. There are governments and leaders who want them for their own selfish purposes and would kill to get them.

The human body was designed and genetically engineered by aliens. This is even written in many books, which includes the Holy Bible. They are the aliens who placed our souls in the bodies they engineered here on Earth from Home. There are those humans who have attempted and are attempting to explain life in terms related to evolution of the species. There is no link between humans and any other animal on Earth.

There are many theories and practices which are blindly accepted by some as reasonable explanations of life, and that there is no such thing as a soul or an after-life existence. EHMR continued, "I tell you now that humans have souls, or spirits if you wish, and that the soul is given to humans at conception. When you are conceived you receive a soul. You are then starting your journey of development. Your body is developing as we designed it to do. When birth takes place, you take your first breath of air, and you are then on another step through life, which ends in the demise of the body, but the soul lives on. You cannot escape this end. Humans will develop their minds and souls under the influences of their life experiences. Some will permit evil to control their thoughts and actions, while others will be compassionate, honest and moral. Each human was given the gift of free will at conception.

"Many may find being lazy, greedy, immoral, uncaring, and slovenly is comfortable for them while here on Earth, but will find their reward is endless isolation from their Home. Your gift of free will is not interfered with by us. You make your own choices, good or evil, which determines your destiny. Each human knows within themselves what they are doing."

EHMR seemed very stern to me. He was like a teacher, sometimes repeating the same thing over and over to make sure I understood what he meant. He even informed that he was teaching me these thing so I could use them in accomplishing my mission. There was no humor emanating from him, or at least none that I could detect. I asked him, "Is there, what we call here on Earth – humor – present in your world?"

He replied, "There is great humor in our world. There is also great pleasure which is far beyond what you have here on Earth. In my world the concept of the absence of evil is in and of itself humor. On Earth, humor is generally associated with the ill fortune and grief of another, even going to that other's appearance. That concept of humor, at least to us, is repugnant, ill-conceived and unfortunate."

I felt EHMR was reading my mind, and felt admonished for noticing his appearance, which was different from mine. I wondered if he thought I looked somewhat strange. I tried to control my thoughts, but doubt if I was being successful. I was having difficulty concentrating because I had so many questions. I was also very uneasy. I felt as though I was in a dreamlike state, and realized I had made a promise to perform a mission for an entity named EHMR. I wanted to get away from there, but at the same time I was compelled to find out more.

I was certain beyond any doubt that at that moment EHMR was totally and completely aware of my thoughts and apprehension. He said, "I am now going to transmit information to you that you will use later, but can divulge to no one. You will not have to ask me any more questions, for I know them already. This transmission is not verbal, it is telepathic, as you would believe, and is now done. It is time you now depart from this area and begin your mission. Do not return to this location unless I give you permission to do so, and do not reveal it to any other human unless I give you permission to do so.

"You will perform this mission with great haste. It is the most serious thing you can ever do. I trust you will keep your promise to me, and I will know when you do.

"If you should endeavor to write this down, you must do it yourself. You can have no other humans assist you. You will use the simplest form of your language, and articulate nothing. You will write everything in the same manner as I have spoken to you. You shall add nothing and take nothing away. You will not divulge to anyone those things I have told you not to divulge until such time as I authorize you to do so. Those things are for your benefit to complete your mission, and in moments of doubt, which you will have, will give you faith. You will keep it that way until I tell you differently. Do you understand that this is our agreement?" I said that I understood.

He now wanted me to go, and had just told me so. He said he had answered all of the questions I had for him. But there was something important I had to find out. He said he had come here in a spaceship, but I could not see it, and wondered where it was. I was curious as to where it was. Was it so high in the sky that I could not see it or was it hidden nearby? I wanted to find out where it was and what it looked like. I got up enough courage and said to EHMR, "I have one more request. I know you told me previously that I could not see the spaceship you came to Earth on, but I would like to see your spaceship. May I?"

He looked at me for what seemed a long time, but was probably just seconds, then said, "Yes. It is right near us, but you have been unable to see it. I will take you aboard it now." Out of the corner of my eye there suddenly appeared this giant craft. It was about 300 feet from us. It was huge, and it was beautiful. It was hovering noiselessly about 30 feet above the ground. There was a fluid-like looking "escalator" reaching from the spacecraft to the ground. EHMR told me to follow him. We walked to that escalator and stepped into it. There we no steps and we did not walk up. We were just quickly inside the craft. He told me to touch nothing and say nothing. We were standing in a large compartment, and I got the feeling there were many more, but I don't know how many because that was the only place I was permitted to be in. There were "people," all looking similar to EHMR, some shorter, some taller, but all of them were thin. Each of these people was standing in front of a dome-like structure protruding from the floor. Their backs were turned toward me. They were slightly bent over with their faces placed into an indentation at the top of that dome. The indentation concealed their entire face. There was absolutely no movement from any of them, but I felt they were all busy. There were no chairs or benches in that compartment – no place to sit. There was nothing but those domes. There was no noise. It was totally without sound. My footsteps made no sound.

I looked up at what I thought was the ceiling. It looked weird. I had never seen anything like that before, even in science fiction movies. EHMR then sent me a message that it was time to go. I had really wanted to go to other parts of this craft, but was denied that opportunity. All I got were those few moments. He then moved to the escalator and I followed him down to the ground. He walked with me to my vehicle without any communication to me. I do not recall if I had any questions or not. I do know I was completely dumbfounded. We got to the front of my vehicle and I turned to take another look at the spaceship, but there was nothing there. It was gone as quickly as it had appeared. EHMR stood in front of me for just a moment and said nothing. Then he was gone! I was alone!

I stood frozen in my tracks for a few minutes, staring into the desert where only seconds before had been a giant, magnificent spaceship. Now there was nothing there but the desert and the sparse vegetation and the fence. There was the fence which was there when I arrived, but when EHMR and I walked into the desert to get to the spacecraft, there was no fence, nor was there one when we returned to my vehicle. It was sure there now, though. I walked up to the fence then, hesitant about crossing it. I slipped my body through the wires and followed the footprints EHMR and I left in the sandy soil to where the spacecraft had been hovering. I could see where our footprints stopped, and our return footprints. There was no other evidence that there ever was a spacecraft there. I recalled he had a shadow – I saw it right beside my own. I knew then that I was not imagining this.

I made my way back across the fence and as I was approaching my car I could hear the approach of another vehicle. I was somewhat concerned that this was some security vehicle coming to investigate me for crossing that fence, but it was just another car.

While I waited for the vehicle to pass by, many thoughts rushed through my mind. The first of those thoughts was – *Was this real? Did this really happen?* I thought about the telepathic transmission of information EHMR had made to me. It was the only time he deliberately did this when I was completely aware it was going to happen. That transmission was done instantly and I could feel it and knew what he transmitted.

The vehicle that had been approaching slowed as it passed, and the occupants looked at me and my vehicle parked in the turnout. They were apparently satisfied that all was well and continued on their way. I got into my vehicle and proceeded onto the highway toward Las Vegas.

When I got to Vegas, I went to the hotel and directly to my room, expecting the key to the room would not fit, or that I really did not have a room, and would wake up from sleep soon. Nothing like that happened. The key worked – I had a room. Entering, I went immediately to the bathroom and looked into the mirror – it was me – I was there all alone. There was no one else there. I looked terrible. I guess I really did look that bad and wondered if I looked like that all of the time during the meeting with EHMR.

I sat down at the small table near the window in my room and pondered this day. What should I do? I had no answers for myself. I did not know what I was going to do. I turned on the TV and watched something for a short while, but I don't remember what it was and didn't care. I guess it was only to have some noise. I was so stressed I could not concentrate and did not want to sit in that room any longer. I quickly changed clothing and headed down to the bar for a much-needed drink. On my way to the bar, a thought struck me, *I wonder if I had been appropriately dressed for this meeting with EHMR?*

CHAPTER 9
SEARCHING FOR A SOLUTION

The bar was pretty well packed. I thought to myself that now I could begin referring to people as people again, instead of as humans. I stood around watching the gamblers out on the floor for a few minutes waiting to catch an open spot at the bar in case someone left. Soon a guy left and I grabbed his seat. That was one busy bar. Each seat had a video poker game implanted into the bar top. I had a quarter-game in front of me. Each person there had that expectant winner's look on their faces with each new set of coins. Some of the people seemed to be truly enjoying themselves, while others had that look of desperation: If I don't win, I starve.

I sat there for a while before a bartender came by. He politely asked what he could do for me. I said I would like a Johnny Walker Black with two pinches of ice chips and a splash of soda. He asked if I wanted quarters, because if I did then the drink would be on the house. I said that sounded like a pretty good deal, and asked for two rolls. Soon he was back with my $20 worth of quarters and my drink. I sat there for a few moments sipping on my drink, unrolling the quarters and putting them into the coin slot.

While doing this the thought struck me – *Where did EHMR go when he left me out on that desolate highway? Did he go home? Or, is he permanently there at that location? Do he and all those other aliens live here permanently, or do they commute to and from work daily?* I did not ask EHMR these questions which seem so simple now, while I had the opportunity, and he did not offer any information.

It didn't take long for me to go through the first roll of coins. I had also finished my drink. I summoned the bartender to bring another drink, and then started on the second roll of coins. By the time the bartender returned with my drink those coins were gone. I sat there slowly sipping my drink and watching the crowd on the casino floor. It was noisy at the casino and I could not relax or think. It was time I do some real thinking in a more quiet atmosphere.

I left the casino and caught a cab, requesting that I be taken somewhere that had good food and was quiet. He knew just the place, and took me to an Irish pub. It was quiet and a much more relaxed atmosphere. I sat at a booth and ordered my dinner and another drink.

While waiting for my dinner to arrive, I sipped my cocktail and reminisced on the events of the day. I looked around at the patrons to see if EHMR might be there having dinner and watching me. Was I getting a complex, or what? Of course he wasn't there. I just had to look, though.

EHMR and I had "talked" a lot about God and Satan and numbers and souls. He was so emphatic about the concept of souls of humans and the rehabilitation of all of the people on Earth to return to their Home that it made me think his only mission here was to get all of us back Home, wherever that is. EHMR said that was his only purpose in being here. If EHMR was right, then there is only one concept of Heaven and only one way to get Home so you can join into God's plan. Why then are there so many concepts of Heaven and how to get there? There is greed, anger, jealousy, hate, envy, deceit, lies and rage in great abundance throughout the Earth, even around the corner at your best friend's home or even closer than that. Based on what EHMR told me, this is not in God's plan.

Recalling EHMR had said there was no religion on Earth today that is correct, I realized just how powerful a weapon the concept of religion is when placed in the hands of selfish, self-serving humans.

There is a mammoth difference between religion and faith. Today most people misplace their faith into the hands of religious leaders who then control their thinking and what those religious leaders desire them to become. The religious leaders change and corrupt the Law of God, then teach it as if God intended it to be that way. They tell us that their teachings are the only way to Heaven, and that religious leader can forgive you your sins.

According to EHMR there is no living person on Earth who can do that. Each of us must use our free will and make our own decisions. To go to God, a person must be honest and sincere, because God knows when you are not, and any words one may pray mean nothing to God unless you are honest and sincere. The final decision of whether or not one returns Home lies in each human's self-control, not in the hands of others.

This triggered my memory of a conversation I had had with an Iranian military officer (a self-professed Christian) several years ago. He related this story to me. It was during the Iran-Iraq war. He was on the front lines directing an Iranian infantry assault on an Iraqi position. It was heavily defended. The approach was defended with massive minefields placed by the Iraqis. The Iranians were unable to penetrate the minefields for several days and were being pressed by their commanders to get the assault going again. Lacking the necessary equipment to clear the minefields, it was determined they would use animals, such as chickens, cows, donkeys and any other animal that could walk to clear them. As they forced these animals into the minefields and the explosions began, the animals balked and refused to enter that area regardless of the provocation they used to get them to enter. They could not be pulled, pushed or forcibly driven out there.

Finally in desperation, the officers developed a plan. They mustered the Iranian twelve- and thirteen-year-olds to hear readings from the Koran and a speech by one of the officers. Their attention was then directed to a structure surrounded by green trees and shrubs several hundred yards on the opposite side of the minefield. They were told that if they could reach that structure they would go immediately to Heaven. They were told there would be no more war for them, but they had to reach the structure. Oddly enough, every one of the children was eager to participate. They were then lined up along the minefield and directed to charge toward that structure. In frantic waves they charged across, oblivious to the exploding mines and the accompanying mayhem and death around them. Most were killed in the rush to be first to the structure and Heaven.

There was now a fairly safe path through the minefield, and the Iranian units moved on to a successful assault on the Iraqi position. The young soldiers who made it to the structure were placed back into the regular service. I wondered if there may have been some disappointment that they had not been taken directly to Heaven as promised.

Enough of this morbid pondering, I thought to myself. I finished my dinner and went back to the hotel. I took a shower and went to bed, thinking that tomorrow would be a better day to decide what I was going to do next, if anything. I lay in bed thinking, *I made a promise to EHMR, and now it all seems so unreal. What am I doing here? I will make some kind of plan tomorrow, I sure can't think about that now.*

Awakening the next morning, I looked at the clock. It was just a few minutes past eight. There had been no messages from EHMR, nor any indication he even existed. There was no feeling of a "presence." I got dressed and went to the restaurant in the hotel for breakfast. I had a feeling I should get a plan in order so that I would know what I was going to do next and when I would do it.

Upon my return to the room, I sat down with a note pad and pen in hand. *Now I will figure this out,* I thought to myself. I attempted to jot down some of the high points of my contact with EHMR. I kept being interrupted with the realization that this encounter had taken place just as I had been told that it would. I had not been hallucinating or dreaming or imagining all of the previous "voice" and "presence" contacts. They were real and I had seen him, touched him and been aboard a spacecraft with him. He had taken me traveling and I had been through a dimensional change with him. I wondered if anyone would believe this if I told tell them. I had my doubts.

My mind was a jumble of thoughts. I had no pictures, no evidence, no tapes, nothing – just a memory of a verbal, physical and telepathic encounter. I could not even disclose where the meeting had taken place and could not revisit that location unless I had the prior approval of EHMR. Therefore I could not even take someone to that location to show the footprints in the sand. I was promised though, that he would always be with me if I should need him. Well, I needed him now. It was a strange thought, for at that moment, all of our conversations and traveling and sights came back as though I was right there again. And I knew then that I would have no problem recalling every conversation word-for-word when I needed it. I realized that no one would believe my story of a meeting with an extraterrestrial, an alien, who was peaceful, intelligent far beyond the imagination of the smartest man or woman on Earth, and was real. I began to accept the fact that I would be ridiculed.

I wrote down a few options that were available to me. First, I could contact those who have had UFO experiences and those who have had extraterrestrial contact. Second, I could go to a TV or radio station and see what they could do with this. My last option was to write about it myself. I did not have a lot of options open to me. I had been told by EHMR to tell or write my experience as directed in the simplest form. I did not want to mix my experience with others and did not want to be influenced by others as to what had just happened. I was directed not to embellish on this or take anything away from it. And, I was to locate sixteen people who would help me with this mission. It was logical that I should find those people first.

I realized that it would take a lot of time, money, and research to locate many of the people who acknowledged UFO and extraterrestrial contact, but it seemed logical to attempt to contact them first. Why not? They would at least understand what I was going through and possibly could give me some moral support. After all, they had already been there and were not afraid to publicly announce their experiences. I recalled that many of them had incurred some serious adverse public opinion cast upon them.

I recalled that several years ago I had visited a place in Yucca Valley near Palm Springs called Giant Rock, and had eaten in the restaurant there. The walls of the restaurant were covered with pictures of UFOs and people who had contact. It had become rather well-known because of its annual UFO convention. I had never been to one of the conventions and had no interest in going, but had read about the conventions in the newspapers where it was reported that over 12,000 attended annually. I felt that would be a good place to start. Further, it would be difficult for me to tell my story. The more I thought about it the clearer it became just how difficult this would be. I knew I was going to have to just shoot from the hip. I made the decision that I would drive out there the next day.

The next day I was out of Las Vegas heading toward Palm Springs when I realized I had made a commitment to EHMR and was now actually planning to conduct a search for sixteen people located somewhere on Earth. I didn't even know what those sixteen people would contribute. This whole thing seemed like a dream to me now. It was beginning to take on the image of science fiction in my mind. I knew it was not, even though it seemed impossible. I began to think that this would be okay if I just tried to do something, but felt that I probably would not be able to locate even one person. I knew I had made the commitment to do this totally. That, I knew, was reality.

As I approached the I-10 interchange to Palm Springs, thoughts of how to handle this were all I could think about. It was now only about one hour away from my planned destination, Giant Rock. I arrived in Yucca Valley with plenty of daylight remaining, so I took the road from there toward Giant Rock on a dusty, rough, old road named Washer Woman Road. As I meandered along, I thought to myself that if I could just get in contact with enough of the UFO advocates and believers, it would make my task much easier to get others involved in this search, as well as to get this message from EHMR out as I promised. I realized I would be required to relate the entire story to whomever I talked with. Just bits and pieces of this story would not work. Besides that, EHMR told me to relate the story from beginning to end.

It was striking me now that this was going to be an all-consuming task, and the magnitude of it was just beginning to set in. I thought, *How am I going to do this?* The reality hit me – there were two tasks. One was to get EHMR's message out to as many humans as possible, and the other was to find the sixteen. Shortly after these thoughts were clearly implanted in my mind, my task became greater. I came upon a barbed wire fence strung across the road with a large sign hanging on it which stated: ROAD CLOSED- U.S. GOVERNMENT PROPERTY-NO TRESPASSING. I was near Giant Rock but could not see it. I thought that I might have gotten my directions confused and this was not the right way.

I turned my vehicle around and returned to Yucca Valley where I stopped at a convenience store. I went inside and asked the cashier if he could give me directions to Giant Rock. He told me that the government had taken it over and closed part of the road. I would have to take another road to get there. He gave me some complicated directions and said the restaurant was still there and operating. My only concern was the UFO convention.

I asked him if he knew what happened to the UFO convention that was held there annually. He said it had moved somewhere in the Midwest, but he didn't know where. I thanked him for the information and headed to Palm Springs. I realized I had some more planning to do, if you could even call it planning.

This thing was now turning into something that was, in my mind at least, a confusing and probably impossible task. As I drove I attempted to come to grips with the problem confronting me. I recalled that EHMR had stated that this was all I had to do. So, to a super-intelligent extraterrestrial, this is simple, but it was not simple for me. I reminisced on some of the things EHMR had told me. He told me that humans were not properly using their minds, or the things that are on Earth. I felt quite strongly at this point that he was right, especially in my case right now. Realizing that I would have to get my mind absolutely clear to get this done, I resolved that I would try total concentration that evening and night in the motel.

My vehicle moving along at about 55 miles per hour brought to mind another matter EHMR discussed with me. He told me that humans had not properly harnessed the energy sources available to them. I listened to the engine in my vehicle and thought that was purring along pretty good. I liked the sound it made. Besides that, there were few other options available for us to travel distances in a reasonable time. EHMR told me of the power of gravity, that it has several forms and can easily be harnessed. Once mankind figures out how to capture the powers of energy and gravity, there would be an inexhaustible energy source available, as well as many other benefits that we cannot even imagine. He told me that the three UFOs I had seen use this source of energy.

I was now in Palm Springs and proceeded to the motel I had selected. I checked in and went to my room and sat quietly for a while, just to think of the days events. I was not pleased with them at all. I felt I was awash in a storm-filled ocean. I began concentrating on a possible plan of action. My thoughts wandered from one subject to another. My concentration was gone. I did not have it, at least right then.

I walked to a nearby restaurant and ordered dinner. As I was sitting there awaiting the arrival of my dinner, the thought came to me that I had better make a real good record of all the conversations I had with EHMR, simply because I was still unsure if I could recall them properly. After dinner I returned to my motel room and began writing. The first things I thought of writing down were the very things that EHMR told me I could not divulge to anyone at any time unless I had his explicit permission to do so. There were a lot of those. So, after destroying those notes, I began writing down those parts of conversations that I could divulge.

One of the things that I recalled was, "A righteous nation develops many righteous people. Your environment affects how you live, act, and think. An evil nation develops many evil people. People individually create a righteous nation, and return Home individually. Leave evil behind and never look back." That statement was made by EHMR while he was telling me about the prison colonies. He also stated that two nations returned to their Home planet, that they had all gone Home at the same time, the souls of the dead and the living alike. That was when I inquired of him if I was qualified to go Home. He answered by saying that choice is an individual thing left entirely to the exercise of one's free will. I did not pursue it further because I had the feeling he was not going to answer it, but I wish I had. I would like to know.

I jotted down as many notes as I could that evening. I had to get some kind of a plan going. I worked on that for a while and really didn't have anything that was worth the paper it was written on. Again, I tried to sit and attempted to concentration on this subject. It was difficult. I kept coming up with writing everything down in letter form and sending it to as many people as possible. But I had no idea of who they would be. That, in and of itself, could be a mammoth job. The idea of putting it in book form was not appealing to me at all. It kept creeping back into my thoughts though. The easiest and most palatable idea was just to contact a lot of people, or so it seemed to me at the moment. I realized this would take quite a bit of time, but I would have to deal with that. There was no other way. I could not rush this. I was quite apprehensive about doing this now. I decided I would take my time at it, if I would do it at all.

Several months had now passed and I had done nothing more than think about what I was going to do someday. There had been no more contact from EHMR or any others. I had discussed this with no one. Quite frankly, I was afraid to bring this subject up to anyone. I was beginning to think I was just too lazy to do this. I would do it tomorrow. There were too many tomorrows coming at me. I wondered where I would be tomorrow when the sun sets on me.

Well over a year had passed now, and I had done nothing. I had contacted no one at all, nor discussed this with anyone. Then one day I was sitting in my living room watching television. It was a re-run of a game show I had seen before. Suddenly, the urging was upon me. No words – just an impression that I was not alone. And then a message in the form of a question: Why wasn't I doing what I had promised? It was back again! I determined that I would start on this soon.

Another year went by, and I still had done nothing. There sure are a lot of tomorrows in a year, and I was looking ahead to more of them. I was really becoming determined not to do this and as each tomorrow passed I became more determined. It also became easier to put off as each day passed.

I was driving with my good friend to a nearby town and we started discussing UFOs and extraterrestrial existence. I brought up the subject of my encounter – not in detail though, just vaguely. He became very interested and urged me to reveal more. I told him there were only certain things I could reveal, but would write those down as the events had unfolded, and as I had been directed to do by EHMR. It became quite lengthy. Still, in all, it was at best a half-hearted effort – and time-consuming. I knew I was just procrastinating. I was so used to procrastinating that I would even put procrastinating off until the next day.

I really thought I had this thing beat and was not going to do it at all. That was until one night several months later, when I was awakened out of my sleep by a brilliant light completely engulfing my entire bedroom. There was EHMR! He was standing beside my bed. He said to me, "You have not fulfilled your promise to me. I have done what I can to help you, and I am here now to help you. You will write down all of the events that I instructed you to. You will disseminate them soon. You will do this. You will keep your promise to me. You will begin now."

The brilliant light and EHMR were then gone. I was sitting up in bed. I was not blinded by the light, but I was shaken by EHMR's appearance. I thought I was out of the woods on keeping my promise. I was not and realized it. I was going to write this story. I had to write it. I would locate the sixteen people as per EHMR's directions and instructions. While writing this I realized I would have to I locate the sixteen and had no idea how seeing their numbers worked. That was a stumbling block. But, I went to work with a new vigor thinking that the answer to this puzzle might clear up as I went along.

CHAPTER 10
COMPLETING THE BOOK

Writing the book was one of the most difficult tasks I had ever undertaken. I had quite an extensive background in writing documents, event histories, and some stories, but now I was dealing with a mystical personal experience. I experienced many story starts, but none of them seemed to be quite right and failed to express my feelings. So I decided I would just charge headlong into this and get it done. That is what I did. I titled the book *To Earth with Love.*

I wanted to get this mission complete (get his message out to as many humans as possible telling them that they must rehabilitate themselves) and get EHMR gone from me forever. After all, he told me that this was all I had to do. I felt that I would then return to a normal life, and not have to concern myself further with the "presence," "Voice," or EHMR. I was sure they would have other things to do in other places with other humans.

I was living in Pahrump, Nevada (a small town a few miles north of Las Vegas). It is a quiet little town with casinos as its primary industry. There are many wonderful people living there, most with the intent to have a nice, pleasant environment in which to raise their families or retire. Others commute to Las Vegas daily to work. We met the most wonderful and unforgettable people in our lives there and will always cherish their friendship.

I worked long and hard, but the writing was slow going, primarily because we had so many other things we were doing. I began procrastinating when I was about halfway through writing the book.

That continued until I even completely put it away for months at a time. Then one night while sitting in my bed wide awake, I received another visit from EHMR. It was similar to the last visit I had from him. The bedroom was suddenly filled with a brilliant light and then EHMR appeared standing at the foot of my bed. He looked directly at me and said, "You must complete your mission. That is your promise to me. I want you to get the book completed so you can complete this mission. It is most important that you do so." I asked him if he would tell me more about the sixteen and my ability to see people's numbers, because I did not understand them. He told me that he would not at this time because it was not important for me to complete writing the book, but that he would tell me more later. He was then gone – so was the brilliant light.

I looked over at my wife who was still sound asleep, and awoke her. I asked her if she had seen the bright light – she said she had not.

We discussed this for some time that night, and agreed that I would have to finish the book quickly. The next morning I was back working diligently on the book and kept that pace until it was complete. Now came the chore of getting it published and out to as many people as possible. Believe me: getting a book published is a lot of work. It is a huge task that is filled with frustration, disappointment and discouragement. I persisted and finally got it published. At first this seemed like the final hurdle, but it wasn't. It was merely part of the first step.

Now I had to get the word of my mission out. It doesn't do any good just sitting on a shelf. I wanted people to read it and its message. I was invited to be a guest on a TV channel. That did generate some interest. I found out for sure there were a lot more people in every community who believed in UFOs and extraterrestrial existence than I had imagined. I found there were many people who contacted me, who had had their own experiences, but would divulge them to no one. They did tell me their stories because they felt I could be trusted to keep their names anonymous – which I do. They were, for the most part, concerned about their jobs and reputations. I really do understand their positions.

Others contacted me but had the opinion that the experiences I had were no more than my imagination. I want everyone to know that I appreciate those points of view as well as the points of view of those who agree with part or all of the experiences that I divulged in the book. Both camps had questions which I answered from my point of view. I was careful not to contradict their opinions. I found out one thing, though. I felt no anger or resentment toward anyone who had a valid question or disagreement with me. Personal attacks, of course, are something else, and those are simply ignored. I have found that this type of attack comes from those filled with self-hate, doubt, and anger, or those who do not want their status quo disturbed. In any event, I related only what EHMR told me I was to say.

There are others who argue that this is about religion. I would like you to know that this is not about religion – it is about faith. There is a great difference between religion and faith. Just think about it – there are hundreds of religions that all believe in a creative force or intelligence. Faith is a belief in that creative force or intelligence, and knowing that it is God. Religions are simply various groups that practice getting the rewards of their faith in that mysterious Creator through various teachings selected by the leaders of that religious group. The reward is called Heaven.

I am talking about an alien (an extraterrestrial being) who told me that humans have souls, and that after we pass from this Earth – all that is left is the soul. We started with just a soul. If you do not nourish the soul as God has directed, you cannot return to Heaven, or as EHMR called it, Home. You must be cautious that the teachings you receive are proper. Our purpose on Earth is simply the opportunity to return Home. The only way to return Home is through God's Law, not man's. There is no other purpose for us being here.

I am only talking about extraterrestrial beings, UFOs, ghosts, spirits, souls and unexplainable supernatural phenomena, none of which can be explained in the conventional wisdom as exercised here on Earth today.

I have asked myself these questions and am now going to ask you to think about them. Possibly you have an answer or theory that would clarify things for all of us. Is the elusive and mysterious nature of the soul similar to the elusive and mysterious nature of UFOs, extraterrestrial beings, the appearance of ghosts, souls and aliens? Does it sound similar? How can one deny the existence of any one of these, but accept others?

If you were in your church or at your home praying to an invisible God, and the misty image of a ghost appeared to you, would you be frightened by that appearance? Or, if you were standing in the middle of a cornfield in Iowa and a UFO suddenly appeared near you, would you be frightened? Would you believe it was possible or impossible? Would you think you were hallucinating? When you arrived at you home and were asked, "How did your day go?" would you respond by saying that it was just fine except you almost got run over by a UFO?

Which of these events would you choose to believe to be real or possible? Would that be because of your environment and teachings? Has your priest, rabbi, cleric or minister ever seen God, Jesus Christ, a ghost, a spirit, a UFO, an extraterrestrial being or a soul? They probably have not because if they would admit to witnessing such phenomena as that, they would fear being classified as a weirdo. Further, this would be a step away from the conventional religion and thinking of the modern civilizations.

CHAPTER 11
OFFER TO GO HOME

The book was now complete and I felt I had done what I could to get EHMR's message out. I did not feel what I had done was much, but what else could I do? There were no further contacts from EHMR so I felt he must be satisfied.

Then on the night of July 28, 1998, at 2 a.m., I was jolted from sleep by two firm hits to my shoulder from my side of the bed, like someone hitting me on the back of the shoulder with the palm of their hand. I sat up quickly and looked around the room to see if there was someone there. There was no one there except my wife, who was sleeping soundly on her side of the bed. I had received jolts like that before, but there was never anyone there. On several occasions, I even searched the house and checked with our son to inquire if he had just done that to my shoulder. He had always been sound asleep, also.

But this time it was different. Shortly after I sat up, a brilliant light filled the room. I knew what it was. I had seen it before. EHMR appeared as if from nowhere. He stood at the foot of my bed. I looked at my wife, and could see her sleeping soundly. She made no movement, nor did she awaken.

He looked at me for a moment, then told me that I had fulfilled my part of the promise I had made to him. I was a little taken by surprise, not only by him appearing in my bedroom, but I was totally unaware of the "my part of the promise" he made in that statement. I did not recall that he had ever made a promise to me of anything in return for me performing that mission. I wondered if it was when he told me that he would always be nearby? Did that mean if I needed help he would be there? I had absolutely no idea.

He stood looking at me for some time after making that statement. I did not know what to say, so I just sat there silently. It seemed like a long time passed, then he asked, "Would you like to see Home?" I jumped quickly from my bed and stood in front of him. *Seeing Home,* I thought to myself, *is my greatest curiosity. Does it really exist?* As I stood there staring at him another thought crossed my mind, *When you go Home do you have to pass from this life? You should not be among the living in the familiar sense we know it.* I looked around and do not know if I pinched myself or not, but realized I was among the living. I did not respond to his question.

He said that I had nothing to fear. He was not going to harm me and no harm would come to me. I recalled that he had made that statement to me before and nothing had happened to me. He had consistently reassured me that he was not present to harm anyone. But now, I was being required to make a quick decision on a totally unexpected question.

I did not respond to EHMR immediately. I had to think about this. I knew that all I had to say was yes or no. *What was home like?* I kept asking myself. This was something that I had wanted to see and now the opportunity was presented to me, and I was having a problem making a decision. I thought to myself, *I am going to do this,* and told him that I would very much like to see Home, and that I would go.

Without any further communication he turned toward the northeast corner the room which led out to the backyard. There was no longer the wall of the room in front of us. There had been two windows, one on each side of the corner before; now there was not even the wall – it was wide open as though that wall never existed. I could see clearly out at everything. There was a small craft hovering in the vacant lot next to my home. It appeared to be about the same size and color of the three craft my friend and I observed near Palm Springs. I looked back at my sleeping wife. She had not moved, and I was not in bed. The blanket and sheets were visible where I had tossed them off when I jumped out of bed.

We walked to that craft right through the opening where just moments before a wall had been. As we approached closer to the craft I looked back at my home wondering if the hole in the wall was going to remain there. There was no longer a hole there – my house was totally intact.

I was taken aboard in a like manner as the first time I went aboard at the first meeting with EHMR. I could see no windows in the craft from outside, but inside I could see out through what appeared to me to be glass extending from the floor to the ceiling and the entire length of the room in one solid piece. I do not know what it was, but it was one-way. I was in a small room. I do not know if there were any other aliens aboard, but there were none present in that room. I do not know what was in the other rooms. There were no chairs or places to sit. We stood.

The ceiling was again similar to that of the huge craft I had been taken aboard by EHMR. It had straight lines going in all directions, circles at all angles and of various sizes and globes of small lights of various sizes that extended upward through these, and left the impression that there was no beginning or end to this ceiling.

EHMR informed me that we would be moving away from Earth at 37 and one-half degrees left of true North and 47 degrees elevation from the surface of the Earth. There were no commands of, "up, up and away," "fasten your seatbelts" or "this is your captain speaking." There was no roar of engines. It was silent. I was standing and felt no surge of speed or the effects of gravity. But I was aware of the departure. I do not know why I was aware of the departure; maybe because I could see out. I'm sure I saw us depart. I knew we were moving rapidly. I was surprised that we were going Home on such a small craft.

I looked out the windows from where I was standing. Earth was not visible – the Sun was not visible. There only appeared to be what looked to me like small lights – all white. The appearance of the ceiling was not even close to being similar to the scene through the window.

I became suddenly very apprehensive. EHMR had not communicated anything to me except the direction we would be moving. I thought, *Maybe I will not return.* Then I thought, *Maybe I am already dead!* There was a flood of other thoughts at the same time. One of those was, *Do I have to be dead in order to return Home?* I wondered if my wife would wake up to a lifeless body lying next to her in the morning. Then I recalled that I had looked back at my wife and the bed as I exited the house, and my body was not there then.

Was I going Home just to "see" or was I going Home to stay? I wondered if there was a difference between "see" and "go," in the thinking of EHMR? Had I misunderstood what he meant?

All of these questions raced through my mind. I was certain that EHMR knew what I was thinking, but he made no response, nor did he give me a feeling of reassurance that everything was going to be okay. There was nothing from him at all. He just stood beside me. I could not tell where or even if he was looking at anything. I wondered to myself, *Why didn't he respond in some manner? Was he testing my ability to make a decision or choice?* I will probably never know the answers, because I had posed those questions to him as near to telepathic communication as I could and received absolutely no response. I was certain he received my thoughts.

Now I had to be absolutely sure. I had been attempting to communicate my thoughts to him telepathically – was it possible I did not have the ability to do that? If he was waiting for me to make a choice, I was now opting not to go Home. So, I thought to myself, *I had better communicate my thoughts directly to him by use of language.* I did not want to go Home right now. Simply put, I was afraid! And I have no shame in telling anyone that I was.

I then said aloud to EHMR that I had changed my mind and wanted to return to my family. Without questioning this request, he said, "We will return now." He did not acknowledge that he knew my thoughts when I attempted to telepathically communicate my questions and concerns to him. But, he responded to my spoken word instantly.

I felt no change of direction, acceleration or deceleration. Shortly, we were back at the vacant lot by my house. I do not know how much time lapsed, but it seemed quick. There was no communication from EHMR. We quickly left the craft without a word and were walking toward my house. I looked around to see if any neighbors were watching this. There were no lights on in any of the homes that I could see. I could see no one standing outside. I was wondering what I would say to them if they did observe this and approach me about it.

As we approached the house, I could clearly see inside. The hole in the wall was there. I could see my wife sleeping in bed, just as she was when we departed. I was not in the bed. We walked into my bedroom. I turned and looked at him standing behind me. The walls were back to normal. I still had a question that I wanted to ask. "What does your name, EHMR, mean," I asked?

He said it means Eternal Holy Mortal Redeemer. He then disappeared without communicating anything further to me.

Everything was back to normal except that I was now standing in the room rather than in bed. I had exited through the bedroom wall with an alien and returned back through it. I sat down on the bed and awakened my wife. She asked me where I was going. I told her what had just taken place, not knowing if she would believe or understand. She understood what had just taken place and wanted to hear more. She is more than a believer – she is a knower.

We sat and discussed for some time what we thought was meant by "see Home" versus "go Home." We concluded that EHMR was just going to let me "see Home," and that I probably would not have had to pass over to do that. But, if it should have been "go Home," quite possibly, I would have had to die. I do not want to die, I really don't. I will fight to stay alive.

I did not know if EHMR was angry with me or not. When he left me at my house he left without further communication. I felt that I had now completed the mission he had given me while, at the same time, I felt that there was a lot more I could have, and should have done. I had this nagging feeling that I would somehow continue this mission on my own, with or without EHMR. I wondered to myself, *Will he ever contact me again? Will he ever give me such an offer again?* I do not know if I would accept that offer or not, but I am really curious about what Home looks like. I told my wife that we were going to keep this experience to ourselves and tell no one.

It was just prior to that event that I met Richard and Kate Mucci in Pahrump, Nevada. They had read my book, *To Earth with Love*, and asked me if I would be a guest on their TV show, *Out There*. I thought about it for a short time, and informed them that I would be pleased to do so. I had some trepidation about going on TV, because I had heard stories of others who had aired their stories in that manner and met with ridicule from the TV host as well as the listening public. I decided that I would face that, no matter what the outcome. I cannot express my appreciation enough to Richard and Kate Mucci (they own and operate a bookstore in Pahrump, Nevada) for the professional and gracious treatment I received. I received an invitation to appear on their show again a year later, and I did so. I have another invitation to appear on their show when this book is published, but I do not know when that will be. They have a website where they post their guest list as well as much more information at crosswynd.com.

I received very favorable responses from people who had questions and called in during the shows. I also had requests from groups to speak at their meetings. I learned then that there were many people who had experiences with UFOs, extraterrestrials and ghosts. I was contacted by people from many countries who had experiences of their own in their countries. Most of them were fearful of criticism if they ever revealed their stories publicly.

CHAPTER 12
EHMR RETURNS

I was quite confident now that I would never hear from EHMR again because, as he said, I had fulfilled the mission contract I had made with him. I further felt that the only one who could change that would be me. I had a sense of relief with this thinking.

Well, that was all well and good, but one day while reminiscing on the events of the past, I decided I would attempt to contact EHMR. Why I would do this is a mystery to me, but I went into a silent and unbroken meditation and sent a message to EHMR. I knew within myself he would get that message. What I didn't know was if he would contact me in return.

It was only a few days later while I was home alone, that I got the feeling there was a "presence" near me. I had had no feeling like that since the night EHMR came to my home and offered me the opportunity to "see Home." It was daytime and I was sitting at my computer. He then appeared to me.

He looked the same. He said nothing to me, just stood looking at me. I had called on him to contact me, and now here he was. I knew it was up to me to say something first. I said, "I contacted you because I feel that I did not complete the mission we agreed that I would perform." I stopped there, hoping for some response from him, but there was none. He waited for me to continue. I then said to him that I felt strongly that I should continue to attempt to get his message out, but it was such a mammoth task and I had such minimal response, that if I were to continue this mission I would need a lot of help from him. I informed him that he had given me some abilities and gifts, but I was unable to use them, probably because I did not fully understand them.

I went on to state that there are many people interested in such a mission, but who did not want to assist because there is so much doubt on Earth that there is really such a God as the Creator. People want a magic God who permits any immorality and sin, and blame Him for any problems that affect their desires. People blame Him if they become seriously ill or injured or when someone dies at a young age. They blame God for wars, droughts, famines, storms, floods and any other calamity that befalls them.

They think they are going to Heaven no matter what they do here on Earth while they live. I also told him that I was not here to save the world, but only to do what small part I could do helping others realize how important their souls are to God. I told him that my intent to begin with was only to tell people that there were UFOs, extraterrestrials and other phenomena – now it had taken on dimensions of religion in the minds of many with whom I talked. This wasn't all of the concerns I had about the mission he had asked me to perform. There were many more which I expressed to him.

He listened to me without interruption. When I finished, he said that he knew I would be unable to stop doing the mission he had given me, because of what he had taught and shown me. He said "we" have always been near you, and "we" will always be near you. He then said that it was my decision to complete the mission, not his, and at this time there was no continuing obligation for me to do that.

I listened carefully. He continued, "Your main problem is that you have discontinued developing your mind. I cannot force you to pursue that. That is completely in your control and is of your own free will, but the rewards are of immeasurable importance. This mission and its benefits will carry through with you, not only here on Earth, but also onto the other steps to Home, even to the final step to the

God. And all of those with you will also find their rewards and benefits on their journey. I urge you, those around you, and those you contact, to never stop seeking knowledge and wisdom. It is available to you, but you must find it."

He asked me, "Is it your intention to continue onward with this mission?" I told him that I was going to do that. He said that I would encounter many obstacles and challenges in my future journey, but that I was not to fight these obstacles and challenges – work through them instead – I would understand this later.

He again informed me that I had no obligation to do so, but if I should at this time reaffirm my decision as he expected that I would, it would be like a new agreement. But this time it was me asking him to help me on a mission. I told him again that I wanted to continue the mission. He said that he accepted this and would help me as much as he was permitted, but that his help to me was limited by the nature of humans' purpose here on Earth. He said he could not direct humans to rehabilitate themselves or interfere with their free will. Further, if I was not going to aggressively pursue this mission, I should tell him now. Again, I told him that I wanted to pursue this in an aggressive manner. I felt he was satisfied with my positive response. He said that I must promise that I will aggressively pursue my original mission. I said, "I promise to aggressively pursue my original mission." He said that he accepted my promise and in return, he would help me accomplish the purpose of that mission with the assistance he was permitted to provide, and that I would now learn much more.

I asked EHMR if he had any suggestions of how I could more easily convey the spiritual meaning of his message. He told me there were many ways, but that one would be to include in a book a section in which I relate the experiences of others and also include some of my own experiences. He said that a book is the best way to get this message out. I was advised by him to inform my wife of any contact

I had with him, because it was very important that I do so, as she was an important part of this mission now. She would know many things of which I have no knowledge. He went no further than that.

I asked him if he could clarify what he meant by the sixteen. He told me that was a mystery I would have to solve on my own. He had given me as much information as he was permitted at that time, and I would have to figure that out myself – but he was not going to go into that any further. But if I should need help in the future, he would be there. He then said that I should never forget that God has a plan, and so does Satan. Beware! God's plan has no loopholes, but Satan's plan does.

He then left. The feeling of his "presence" was also gone.

CHAPTER 13
ROSWELL AND
OTHER EXPERIENCES

I was now sitting alone again in my home. This was the first time that I had been able to send him a message and ask him to appear. He did not appear instantly but did appear. It was also the first time he appeared to me in the daytime, other than at that first meeting in the desert. I realized that I could contact him anytime I wanted to, and he would be aware of it – just that he may not respond.

Now I was committed to writing another book on this matter of getting the message from the aliens for humans to rehabilitate themselves in order to return Home upon their demise from this Earth. At least I must try my best.

I decided to use some of the stories others had told me as well as some of my own experiences. EHMR told me that this was one way to let others know they are not alone in this world with only their own experiences. I began diligently going through these stories. I had a lot of them. Most of the people who wanted me to tell their stories requested I not use their names because they did not want any public ridicule. Others gave me permission to divulge their names with their stories. I agreed to honor their requests.

While researching and getting these stories together, I was also researching other phenomena. The crash of a UFO in Roswell, New Mexico, was of great interest to me. I was not satisfied with the government explanations and cover-ups or the newspaper accounts. The witnesses to this incident were all hushed up by the military which also threw up a smokescreen that was so thin it makes one almost laugh. But it seemed to work for most of the general public. The government simply denied such an event and then kept all of the documents locked up and out of reach of anyone who inquired. The military simply denied there was a UFO and went silent. With all of the documented sightings made from all corners of the Earth dating back to centuries prior to Roswell and many since that crash, it makes one wonder why they would deny such an existence.

I thought that if I ever see EHMR again, I was going to ask him about Roswell, and this time I would insist on more information. I wanted to know if he would tell me what it was about, because if it was a UFO, he should know.

It was only a short time after that that EHMR appeared to me. It was late at night. The room was again brilliantly illuminated and he appeared. He informed me that he would like me to get started more aggressively on the new book. He told me I was lagging and should pursue this project in a more energetic manner.

This was my opportunity to ask him about Roswell. So, I asked him if there really was a UFO crash there and if there were aliens on board that craft. He said he would tell me about that incident, and that I should write it in the book.

This is what he told me: There was a crash of an alien craft at Roswell. It had four occupants inside. It was confiscated by the U.S. government and military. There are attempts being made as we speak to back-engineer the metals that the craft was built of and the energy source that powered it. Those efforts are under the strictest secrecy. The military and other agencies will not permit any of the research being conducted to be public knowledge.

The alien craft we see are far advanced by the conventional standards of humans on Earth, even though they are from our galaxy, the Milky Way. There are six other planets in the Milky Way similar to, but much different from, Earth. Each of these planets has its own distinct atmosphere and physical appearance of its inhabitants. They are all similar, but have been genetically engineered by the aliens to adapt to the environment of the planet they inhabit. The inhabitants of all of the other planets are space travelers and explorers of the universe, but they too are limited, as are the inhabitants of Earth. Their purpose of existence on their planets is the same as humans' existence here on Earth – they too, must rehabilitate themselves in order to return Home.

They, like humans, know there is an intelligent Creator or force, or God as humans call it. They also want to find Home or Heaven, but they cannot. They can only explore what they are able to reach physically and mentally in this galaxy. Home is not within their physical capabilities, and there is only one way that one can go Home, and that standard is firmly established and controlled by God. All things in the universe fall within that standard, even hell, where those souls rejected at Heaven must go when their bodies leave this mundane life. They have also developed their minds beyond what we have attained here on Earth. They have solved the problem of harnessing the forces of the several forms of gravity as a source of energy.

I now had the opportunity to ask EHMR a burning question. "Could the spacecraft you have shown me crash as the one in Roswell did?" He said, "No. They are much different than those we use. They are mechanical, while ours are of a completely different nature. No human or traveler from the other planets is capable of seeing our craft unless we desire them to see them. I am not going to explain any more than that, except to tell you that our craft cannot crash, and that is all I will tell you at this time, because you could not understand it."

I had one more question on this subject and asked him if he would tell me if he was like the occupants of the Roswell spacecraft. He told me that they are not like him or those with him. He said they were similar to humans, but would go no further than that.

I asked him if the souls of humans were capable of true astral projection and travel through the astral planes. He said that some humans have developed their minds and can easily do this. He went on to say that humans could even see and meet God through this mental function, but it would have to be with the permission and assistance of a lesser God, and some people have done so. He said that humans can develop their minds to leave the body and project themselves into other places where they can see that location and its contents as well as "hear" the conversations of the people located there. But to visit God is at His discretion.

He did not say that he was leaving or that this meeting was concluded. He just stopped and looked at me. I told him that I needed to know more about how to find the sixteen. He told me that he had already given me the ability to see a person's number. I had to figure out how it worked because it was simple if I would apply myself. He said that as he had instructed me before that each human has a number assigned at conception, and that number is special to that human forever, but can change based on that person's own free will. He told me that I would identify the number by use of (what I thought, based on his telepathic communication) the number one o1, and that is how I would know their number. More than one person can have the same number, but each number is special to that individual, and even though the numbers may be the same, they are different. He than told me that I would have to work on that if I did not understand it.

He said that he was going to depart, but before he did, he told me to work diligently on the new book. He then departed.

I looked over at my wife. She was still sleeping soundly. I did not even bother to awaken her this time. I went back to sleep, and then discussed this with her the next day. She told me to awaken her the next time I received a visit, and I told her I would.

For the next few weeks I had plenty to think about and do. I jotted down all I had been told that night, especially the Roswell incident and the sixteen thing. I knew now that there are two types of spacecraft – those that could crash and those that could not. I knew that most of the aliens that visited Earth were travelers from the other six planets in our galaxy, and those were the spacecraft we can see here on Earth. The occupants are similar, but different from us. The other type craft cannot be seen by us unless the occupants desire us to see it, and these spacecraft cannot crash.

I now attempted to work out the number issue. This is what I could see when I saw a person's number: 11111111111111111111111111111111111111111111111111. It was like that, except the numbers continue on to what looked like infinity. Then there were two of these numbers that were brighter than the other number ones, and one of them was brighter than the other. It simply made no sense to me. I took it to a trusted friend and asked for his opinion. Neither of us could figure it out. I spent many hours attempting to solve this problem, but was largely unsuccessful.

CHAPTER 14
THE KEY TO THE SIXTEEN

I had been struggling with this problem now for over a month with no solution in sight. I was now becoming convinced that EHMR was right when he told me that I was not very bright. I hoped he meant to mean that humans are not generally capable of truly understanding the power of the human brain because we do not concentrate on fully developing the powers that lie within each of us. I had many pages of diagrams and every conceivable concept that my mind was capable of creating. I was getting nowhere.

It was during that period of time that, quite by accident, that my wife and I met a very sophisticated lady name Christina Piroska through mutual friends. She was introduced to us as a person with psychic abilities. She asked me if I was the Ray Holm she had seen on *Out There* a while back. I told her that I had been on the show as a guest. She then told me something shocking: She had been contacted by EHMR and was told that she was to contact me and deliver a message to me which was – Take two of the books, *To Earth with Love*, and donate them to the public library. She told me that that was the only thing he told her to do. She said that she had attempted to reach me but had been unable to do so.

When we departed I shook her hand and touched her on the shoulder. I felt a great energy emanating from her. I could also see her number, but had no idea what it meant. I stood back and looked at her, wondering just who this lady really was. We agreed to stay in contact. I donated the two books to the public library, but to this day, I do not know why that was important. She is the only other person I have met who has been telepathically contacted by EHMR.

From that day, my wife and I have been close friends with her. And she is very psychic. We learned later in our friendship that she was the prima donna of the original Paris Follies Bergeres in France, her homeland, as well as being a countess in France and Russia. She has taught dance to many of the Follies dancers in Las Vegas. She is truly gifted with insight, and is a pleasure to visit.

I was getting bogged down attempting to write, because I was stuck on the sixteen issue. As this was one of the key issues I needed to understand in order to continue, I was simply unable to proceed. EHMR had told me he would be close by at all times. I guess he must have been watching as well, because one day shortly after the last visit, he appeared to me during the day when I was alone at home. I could feel his "presence" before he appeared. When I felt that "presence" I knew he was near and would make himself visible to me soon. I was not surprised or shocked when he did so.

This time he spoke before I could say anything. He told me that I had almost mastered the understanding of what sixteen meant, and that he was now going to give me the secret to understanding it. He informed me that what I thought were the number ones were not ones at all; they were short horizontal lines (planes), and were not to be viewed set vertically side-by-side on a plane that is horizontal. Instead, they are set horizontally, one above the other. These are the planes on which one's soul is resting. These planes denote the steps to Heaven. Now I could envision this.

I thought of the Bible story of Jacob who discussed a ladder that extended from Earth to Heaven. I inquired of EHMR if this would be similar. He said that I could describe these planes using the term "ladder" if I desired. He said that each human has a ladder that is exactly like all other human ladders. Every person's ladder (number) is exclusively their own. No one else can ever use that ladder.

He told me that each human's number is the number of the step on which your soul (life energy) is residing at any given moment on or above the (positive) Bright Line, with the Bright Line being the first step. The positive energy of one's soul can be seen residing on a step on or above that Bright Line. The brightness you see on that step is that of one's soul. Your positive energy appears on your step as a glowing globe.

You will now see a Bright Line on each of the ladders. That Bright Line is the dividing line between positive and negative. Every sixteenth positive step has a plateau. These are to be referred to as Levels. All human souls start their journey of life on the Bright Line in a body provided and designed by the Creator, and as they advance up the ladder their step is bright, but not as bright as the Bright Line. Humans are essentially on their own as they advance upward on their journey Home.

A human may advance up the steps as far as their positive energy permits. They can only climb higher and higher by developing their minds and the wisdom, knowledge, and understanding accepted and practiced by them in a positive and consistent manner. It is up to each human to do that as much as possible while here on Earth. The human soul's positive energy can be developed only through one emotion – love. This is not to be construed as or interpreted as lust. It means, just to name a few of its qualities and powers, respect of oneself and all other worthy persons, compassion, patience and consideration, moderation in all things one does and charity.

But, charity is the greatest of all, for it lives on long after the donor's life on Earth has ceased. Love also means one is strong, righteous and courageous under the Canopy of God. And that one defends with their life the right to think and exercise their free will. The climb up the ladder is slow and must be consistent with a true knowledge and understanding of love and God's plan.

There are many steps below the Bright Line as well, but these are all negative. To get there is the easiest of all. Laziness, jealousy, greed, deceit, hatred, rage, lust and envy are like an express ticket to hell. Those emotions live exclusively in the domain of Satan. They have no place at Home, and those who harbor any of those emotions as a way of life on Earth will never have the opportunity to meet God.

If one's soul at the time of passing (the soul leaving the body forever) from this Earth should be on the Bright Line, there is still an opportunity for that soul to either live another life on Earth as a human or be directed to the light by them through sincere prayer by the living. If they refuse to go to the light they may wander through the dimensions aimlessly forever. There are many souls that are far above the Bright Line, but feel they have not fulfilled their destinies here on Earth or have a wrong they must right and are reluctant to go Home. Perhaps the soul does not realize that he or she has passed over and is roaming all through the Earth seeking to complete his or her desired goals, but does not understand why these goals cannot be accomplished. Then there are those who are completely neutral in their beliefs and conduct – they are on the Bright Line, neither above it or below it. Their souls too, are wandering the face of Earth. All of these souls still retain their free will.

I was instructed by EHMR that if I should encounter a soul at the third step or lower in the negative zone below the Bright Line, I was to avoid that individual as much as possible.

EHMR then said, "You now understand what is meant by the sixteen. I have given you the ability to see any person's number. When a human's soul rests on the sixteenth positive step of their ladder, they may be accepted by you to actively participate in your mission, but only if they should ask you to permit them to participate. You must not tell any person their number unless they should ask you to do so, nor can you divulge their number to any other person. You shall not write their number down in any form. You may only divulge that person's number to them in proper person and in privacy. They must come to you."

He went on, "There will be many who come to you for their number. Do not waste your time aimlessly. Some will be expecting unreasonable readings. Tell them their true reading. Do not be hesitant in doing this. Also, you may give them direction in rehabilitating themselves. You must be serious when doing this. It is not for entertainment. Many will come to you for this as a form of entertainment. You must establish a forum in which only serious people will come to you for their number. There will be doubters, but do not let this deter you."

Some people may think I am discussing religion. I am not. I was told to tell you this by an extraterrestrial being. I am talking about UFOs, extraterrestrials and other phenomena that is not explainable by conventional scientific methods today. I am talking about the purpose of life on Earth – Why are we here? Where did life and matter originate? Is there a God or more than one God? Are there other dimensions? Is there more than one Universe? Are we alone? Are all of the secrets to life and creation wrapped up in dark matter? These are just some of the things EHMR stated he wanted me to pose to each human on Earth, and let each, using his or her own free will, come to their own conclusions during private and silent meditation. The results from their private and silent meditation help determine their destiny.

There are people who can and do contact the spirits and communicate with them, can and do see into the past and the future. These people are referred to as psychics, seers, clairvoyants or prophets. At the same time, there are many people posing as these gifted people. They are frauds but give themselves these titles. These greedy liars and deceptive frauds are possessed by evil spirits. They prey upon the gullible and destroy many lives. They have learned the terminology of the gifted people and then twist it to their own financial advantage. Of course, there are those who perform a recreational fortune telling service, and if asked, they will tell you up front that they are not psychic, but simply read cards, your astrological charts or palms.

But, worse than that is a false priest, rabbi, cleric, minister, pastor or political leader instilling fear into those who will follow them without question through false and/or superstitious teachings and beliefs, for the sole purpose of profit, power and control. Asking questions and free thinking are not accepted. The intellectual material and education made available to these followers is restricted to meet the ends of those leaders.

Much of religion has been reduced to rituals – no faith or understanding is necessary – just perform the ritual and observe the superstition. If you should ask questions, in all probability you will be admonished and told you cannot question or challenge the Word. But, proper ritual with knowledge, wisdom and understanding is valid.

Have you ever noticed that negative people attract other negative people? They stick together, and remain in groups which do negative things. Then there are positive people who attract other positive people. They remain together and do positive things.

I now see the spiritual energy of people and make my choices of whom I associate with. I have seen energies which are high on the ladder that looks like a glittering ball. It is a beautiful sight. The higher one advances up the ladder, the brighter is the glow of their globe on their step.

I now began hesitantly using the gift of seeing another human's number. I was unsure how to use this without invading their privacy. I did not want to feel guilty about something so sacred to each individual. However, I was told by EHMR that this was the way I would find and determine the people who would help me spread his message to as many humans as possible. EHMR had also told me this would be useful if I should decide to help someone spiritually if they should inquire about their doubts.

They must be at least sixteen steps above the Bright Line on the ladder to be classified as one of the sixteen. However, anyone below the sixteenth step may participate, and I really encourage them to do so. I cannot ask anyone to help in this mission – they must ask and volunteer.

CHAPTER 15
GOD'S LAW AND OTHER STORIES

God created humans and gave the law that governs how we should live our lives in order to return Home. It is called God's Law. It is not to be manipulated, changed or misinterpreted by any human to the advantage of any human. God's Law is constant, steady, unchanging and permanent. God's Law is the cornerstone of God's Plan.

Humans have, through religions, thrown out God's Law and replaced it with their own versions of what God "must have meant" in a massive deception to control the minds, bodies, thinking, money and wealth of others for their own purposes and benefit. God's Law did not change, and is the same right now as it was when he gave the Law. All through these human manipulations and deceptions, it remains steady and constant, and is the same for all humans throughout the Earth. We would have difficulty recognizing God's Law if we would see it as originally given and compare it with the changes humans have made to it over the past few thousand years.

Religion's ideology of politics, economics and mind control have replaced the moral and spiritual faith required by God's Law. Embracing those ideologies will not get you to Home (Heaven). Do you truly believe that a person who kills and destroys the lives of others by a suicide bombing in the name of a political issue, disguised a religious requirement, could go directly to Heaven and possible receive a reward of 72 virgins? Aren't these the same individuals and groups who stone and execute any other people for engaging in any form of sexual activity outside of marriage?

This is not a test, but do you know the Ten Commandments as given by God? Could you readily find them in your home if asked to do so? When was the last time you reviewed them, and when was the last time you broke one of them? Just a thought, but would these same commandments that you find in your home today be the same ones that God gave?

Humans, for some strange reason, think they can change God's Law at their whim or special need – just like special interest groups do with our Constitution and Bill of Rights. Dictators, kings, clerics, priest, ministers, rabbis, presidents, prime ministers and many other people who are in positions of power and leadership use their power and influence to change what you think and learn, as well as how you conduct your life, for their own special interests and/or needs.

There is nothing improper about people with great influence and leadership roles being benevolent and properly dispensing the trust placed in them. There is no sin in people accumulating wealth and influence, so long as that wealth and influence is properly and honestly acquired. Those who do acquire wealth are generally the ones who are most benevolent. They use their wealth not only to better their lifestyles, but also to provide employment and educational opportunities for many others.

It is not within God's Law for any human to deny any other human their due right to respect of self and property by their selfish, greedy and sinful interests. Humans affected by these wrongs may not be able to correct them but by God's Law they will be dealt with at the point of entry into the spiritual domain of God. I did not say this, an alien named EHMR told me that, and further told me to tell each of you that.

I want to clearly state again that I am not anti-government, nor am I anti-religion. I feel very strongly that we need good government, taxation and secrecy in many aspects of government for our own security and well-being. I am pro-government, pro-taxation and pro-faith in an intelligent God.

I am merely stating what EHMR told me is required of us upon our departure from our lives here on Earth before we can return Home. If we do not rehabilitate our souls while here on Earth in our present living form, there is no chance of returning Home in a spiritual form. Everything we do here on Earth is based on a belief in a Creator and willfully performing acts that verify and test those beliefs is our rehabilitation.

We pray and go to the church or attend religious ceremonies many times during our lives. We expect to be rewarded with Heaven upon our demise. When we attend church services, we always dress in a respectful manner to enter that church in honor of God. We must likewise have our souls properly dressed to enter into the Kingdom of God when we pass on. You will not get there if your soul is not properly prepared (dressed) to enter. You will be denied entry. As EHMR told me, "It is up to each of us to individually use our free will to make our afterlife determinations while here in this life."

Religious and political leaders had their thinking housed in a proven concept that has worked successfully for many centuries. That is, if they direct us to think, act, and believe in something over a long period of time, and at the same time deny people the right to any other information or thought (even research), then after generations of such teachings, those teachings become the new law. Everyone accepts these teachings as truth and their children are influenced accordingly, and on and on. This philosophy is human—not God's.

I was told by EHMR that there is no organized religion on Earth today that is teaching the correct way to return Home. Anyone can go to God, but no other human can go for you. Anyone can go to Satan, but no other human will go for you. Each of us has free will.

I am not picking on Catholicism or any other religion. Catholicism was the first Christian church. There was another prominent faith, Judaism, established long before. Then there were the pagans who worshiped anything that moved, could be seen or heard. Hindu and Buddhist faiths had been practiced long before the birth of Christ. But all of these faiths still had an inborn feeling that there was a God. The American Indians worshiped and respected the spirits of their ancestors, of all animals, the sun and Mother Earth.

But, here is what happened to the Sabbath. God clearly directed that man should rest on the seventh day of the week. That day is the Sabbath. God never changed that day.

In about 425 A.D., Emperor Constantine and the pope of the Roman Catholic Church changed that from Saturday to Sunday, the first day of the week. Emperor Constantine made it a law in his Empire that the only religion in his empire was Catholicism and the day of worship was Sunday. The pope issued a decree to all Catholics that the Sabbath was now on Sunday instead of Saturday. It has been so since.

Brutal punishments were dealt out by Constantine and the pope to anyone who did not abide by these decrees and laws. This punishment was dealt out quickly and included torturing and killing.

Emperor Constantine had converted to Catholicism and determined he could expand his empire and would have more control over the many pagans therein if he could convert them to Catholicism. The Roman Catholic Church threw its power behind the emperor to assist him and was looking to increase its membership and sphere of influence. Sunday was the day of the week the pagans held as their day of worship.

Constantine and the pope felt this would now bring the pagans into the Catholic Church. The only problem was that the pagans worshiped idols. The Catholic Church banned the worship of idols based on the Ten Commandments. The pagans were then permitted to worship their idols in the Catholic Church while services were being performed. The Catholics were then permitted to worship idols and graven images also. That practice is carried on to this day.

A problem arose when the pope was later challenged by church members as to who had such authority to change the Sabbath. The problem was explained away quite easily. The explanation was that this is what God would want them to do. Many Christian religions established since then have adopted Sunday as their Sabbath also. Two men, a pope and an emperor, changed God's Law.

Let's look at some of the Commandments. One of them which I am intrigued by is: "Thou shalt have no other Gods before Me." Is there an implication here that there is more than one God, or have I simply misunderstood this? In the catechism of the Roman Catholic Church this has been changed to – "I am the Lord thy God, thou shalt not have strange Gods before me." It has not been clarified what "strange" means.

The Second Commandment is – "Thou shalt make no graven image unto thee or anything that is in the Heaven above." In the catechism of the Roman Catholic Church, this has been changed to and taught as – "Thou shalt not take the name of the Lord thy God in vain." Why would this have been changed and taught? Two men, a pope and an emperor, changed God's Law and justified it by issuing a statement that they had determined that God would want it that way.

The next Commandment I would ask all to think about is: "Thou shalt not kill." Please review the instant foregoing paragraph, and no further discussion is really necessary. It does make one curious if this really was a Commandment, though.

The Old Testament is rich with stories of killing. The great armies even carried God into battle with them. It has not changed from then to now. More people have been killed and murdered, tortured and raped, plundered and robbed in the name of religion than for all other reasons combined.

There exists today, as always has been, terrible jealousy between religious groups and organizations. Many even thrive and prosper on hate. Each claim God is with them only. Does this sound right? How can God be with each of these groups to the exclusion of all others? They kill and destroy those who may believe something slightly different from what they believe, leaving behind only more and deeper hatred, jealousy, rage, greed, looting, envy, enslavement, rape and anger, totally devoid of the only emotion that truly is important – LOVE. Love stands alone and is battered and beaten from all sides. All of the other emotions leave behind a legacy of horror for their victims. I ask, "Is this really in the name of the Lord, God, Jesus, Allah, Buddha or any other deity?" Whatever it is goes on today as it has for thousands of years and will continue until humans awaken.

I am not going into the other Commandments. It is a very touchy subject, but EHMR told me that I should touch on them. I am going to leave that up to each human to research him- or herself. But, I do challenge each person to determine how he or she is going to abide by all of the Commandments and still return Home? Even if one of the Commandments is broken, can you return Home?

This is only my opinion, but I thought there were two great speeches given in the twentieth century. The first was given by Martin Luther King, Jr.: "I have a dream…" The second speech was given by President Bill Clinton: "I did not have sex with that woman…" The speaker in the first speech gave his life for his beliefs, desiring a better life for all people. The speaker in the second speech was only trying to save his own image, and was willing, without conscience, to lie and deceive all of his countrymen and countrywomen.

Which of these public figures would you rather see pass through the pearly gates? Both of these men were eager for power and wealth. Power provides wealth, and wealth provides power. Were they positive or negative?

Now let's take another example. Say that one person told a little "white lie," and another told a "whopper." According to the Ten

Commandments they have each borne false witness. I have searched and searched, but could not find any exception incorporated in the Ten Commandments. They have both told a lie. Humans have taken it upon themselves to make exceptions. They have come up with terminology – little sins and big sins, venial sins and mortal sins. Once humans realized it was quite difficult to live strictly by the Ten Commandments, they made self-serving changes and interpretations to fit their special interests and desires.

During the Dark Ages, the Holy Roman Empire controlled a vast region. There were massive costs with administration of these areas. The church encountered financial problems. To solve these problems they had to raise money. One of the schemes was to sell future indulgences – which meant that if you desired to commit a sin in the future, you simply had to go to the church and request the priest forgive you prior to the act of committing the sin. This was then done promptly by charging a fee for future forgiveness based on the type of sin to be committed.

I am just curious about a few things, and this is one of them. If that priest tried to act like God in selling the indulgence and the purchaser of that indulgence truly believed he was going to be forgiven by God for his act, upon whose soul would the sin rest? Could either of them reach Heaven?

History repeats itself. Today politicians, religious leaders, bankers, stockbrokers and CEOs will promise you anything you want to hear to get your vote, support or money. People want to feel comfortable and let others make their most difficult decisions – personal and business. They will believe whatever appears to be most profitable and comfortable and does not interfere with their leisure time. If something should not go as they had been promised, they blame it on others, never taking responsibility for their feckless acts. I am not saying that one should not trust others, but when one individual or organization promises everyone anything they want, a red flag should go up. If the red flag is not heeded, the results are our own burden to bear.

People must use their free will when making their decisions, and you do this by asking questions, no matter how trivial the question may sound to others. This is your life, your soul.

Other Experiences

I have had many people come to me and ask me if I would include their personal stories in this book. I wanted very much to do exactly that, but there are so many stories that I would not possibly be able to do so. At the urging and direction of EHMR I have incorporated the following stories.

Dawn's Experience

This is her experience as told to me:

I have met God and sat on his lap. I was alone in my bedroom sitting on the foot of my bed one day during a period of time of some turmoil in my life. I was 22 years old. I began praying to Jesus Christ quite fervently asking for his help, when he appeared before me. I was not frightened by his appearance because I knew he existed. He asked me if I would like to meet his Father. I told him that I felt unworthy, but he insisted that I was worthy and should come with him now. He reached out to take my hand. As he touched me, I felt like I was a small child dressed in my favorite green-and-white polka dot dress. He took my hand and we walked slowly up a sun-drenched grassy hill.

As we reached the crest of the hill I could see down the other side into a valley. It was the most beautiful scene I had ever witnessed. It was a city made of crystal, sparkling and glittering with color and light that I cannot describe adequately, because I had never seen such colors or lights before. The sparkle, glittering light and shine were all around the city, and reached high into the sky. There were beautiful mansions along golden-lined streets where people were strolling. It was very calm and peaceful. That city was more beautiful than I can ever put into words. It looked peaceful and serene, and I could feel the peace and serenity. It was overwhelming.

Jesus then said that we were going through two doors. We went through the first door which led to a second door which we then went through. He said, "I want you to meet my Father." I looked directly in front of me, and there sat a huge, white, vibrating figure. I was lifted up onto his lap by Jesus, and He hugged me. I put my arm around Him, and there was the feeling of love and comfort I had never before felt. The love was pure.

I did not want to leave. He told me that He loved me, and that I could come back and visit him anytime that I wanted to. Jesus then said that it was time to go. I said I did not want to go, that I wanted to stay there forever. He said that I could not stay, and must go now, but I could come back anytime that I wished. I reluctantly got down from God's lap, and took the outstretched hand of Jesus. We walked back through those two doors and proceeded back to the top of the hill. As I stood on top of the hill crying, Jesus reassured me that anytime I ever wanted to come back I could do so, but it just wasn't time for me to stay right now.

As we walked across the top of the hill, I took one last look back, and it was just as beautiful as when I had first seen it. As we began the descent to the bottom of the hill, I said, "Thank you Jesus," and gave Him a big hug. Then I turned and ran the rest of the way down the hill alone to my home, and was then back in my room sitting on the foot of my bed.

I will always savor those moments. I did not take lightly God's promise to me that I could come back and visit Him any time I wished. Since that time, I have only been back twice to meet the Father. I go through Jesus to do this. I am now 38 years old, and do not want to abuse this right to visit Jesus and the Father. I am not sure that I could abuse that privilege, but I am careful that I do not, because I never want to lose that privilege.

Each time I have visited, I have never told Him any of my problems, and He has never inquired. All He has ever told me was that I am worthy and could return and visit Him at any time. The problems I had before the visits suddenly seemed as though they were no problems at all. I am able to cope and come up with my own solutions. I know that I can always go back and visit Him because He told me that I could. I know I am worthy.

A Man named Mickey

I knew Mickey. He was a friend of mine. He was quite a wonderful man in his last few years on Earth. I met him in those last few years. He was at one time a very prominent business executive. He was ruthless and cared little about the feelings or well-being of others. He was successful.

During his success he made many friends. He made friends with one very special friend named Cocaine. It kept him going for several years. It was always there for him. He could not do without this constant companion. Then one day his very special friend, Cocaine, made him say something to the wrong person. He encountered some serious physical harm shortly thereafter and had to leave his executive position. He was concerned for his safety and welfare after that, forever looking over his shoulder.

One day, not long ago, when I returned to my home after being gone for several days, there was a message on my answering machine. It was Mickey's wife informing me that Mickey had passed over. His funeral was over before I had returned.

Mickey and I had discussed in detail the message I was given by EHMR. He was excited about the meaning of the message and told me how important he felt it was. He encouraged me to pursue that mission. He said he would like to contribute something to it. He said his contribution would be an experience he had, which paralleled the message I had been asked to deliver by EHMR. He wanted me to include it in this book. We set an appointment for him to relate his experience in detail but something arose and that appointment was canceled. Several other appointments were likewise canceled. I do not know what his experience was, and do regret that I was unable to learn about it.

I prayed for Mickey and his soul several times after his death. One day I got a compelling feeling that I should pray for him right then. I sat back and meditated on this for a few minutes, then began a prayer asking the Lord to forgive his sins. I went deep into meditation and began channeling for Mickey's spirit. I searched and searched. He was really difficult to locate.

I finally located him at a place he used to talk about, Red Rock Canyon, located at the foot of Mt. Charleston near Las Vegas, Nevada. It was sunrise there, even though it was early afternoon in real time. The red rocks were shelved like steps toward the rising sun. I contacted him and told him I was here to pray with him for his sins to be forgiven by God and his soul to be permitted to enter into the realm of God.

He told me that he was not worthy of the realm of God and that he still had some things that he must do and correct here on Earth. I asked him what those things were, and he said that he had to watch over his wife and grandson to be sure they were always protected. But he was very frustrated because he was unable to reach out to them. He felt helpless.

I told him that he must ask the Lord to forgive his sins and that he must get on his knees and bow his head before the Lord to do so. He must be sincere and honest about every aspect of that act. He was reluctant to do so – to say that he was worthy. At that moment the Lord appeared before us with his back to the rising sun and stood looking at Mickey, saying nothing. Mickey, still standing, said to the

Lord, "I am unworthy." The Lord continued to stand there but did not respond.

I then became aggressive in my insistence that Mickey do as I said and must humble himself. I told him that he could do nothing to help his wife or grandson as long as his soul was in its present state. I told him that he must humbly kneel before the Lord right now and sincerely ask for his sins to be forgiven, and that if he did not do so right now the opportunity of this moment may never happen again. I placed my hand on his shoulder and pressed him to his knees beside me. I knelt with him.

Mickey looked into the face of the Lord and said, "Lord, I am not worthy." The Lord stood silent, waiting. Then in the firmest manner I could muster, I told Mickey that he must say he is sorry for his sins, and must ask the Lord to forgive him and allow him to enter into His kingdom and that he must be sincere.

Mickey, again looking at the Lord, said, "My Lord, I am sorry for all of my sins, and know the things I have done were wrong, even while doing them. If you would permit me to enter into Your realm I promise I will do all I can to make God happy."

At that moment I witnessed Mickey's soul go upward two steps and disappear behind the Lord into the beautiful sunrise-washed landscape I had described before. Satan then appeared on the left of this setting and looked at the Lord. Our Lord looked back at Satan and Satan faded away, back to the left from where he had appeared. Satan is terrible looking.

Our Lord looked at me and a bright whiteness came from him and enveloped me momentarily. Our Lord then faded away. Now I was sitting all alone on my living room couch, just as I had been before starting that prayer, except now I was feeling a little tired. This took a lot of energy from me.

It was then that I truly understood what EHMR had taught me – only the Lord can forgive you your sins, and you must ask Him yourself. No one else can ask him for you! I witnessed and participated in this event.

Since that time I have tried to pray for Mickey, but each time I try to pray for him I receive a message. It always is, "You do not have to pray for me anymore. I am just fine. Pray for others." I know Mickey went to Heaven and is now with God. I feel good about that and it makes me feel at peace for him. But at the same time, there is just a bit of a lonely spot in me, as though I had just said goodbye forever to this friend of ours as he left on his voyage into eternal life.

That evening our phone rang. When I answered there was no one there. The caller ID indicated "unknown caller, unknown name." Ten minutes later our fax machine rang and then began what we thought was printing a document. A blank sheet of paper was issued.

A Man named Herman

Herman is my father. The day following my prayer for Mickey, I took my wife to a beauty salon for a hairdo, manicure and pedicure. While she was there, I got a haircut at the adjoining barbershop. I was done long before she was, so instead of sitting idly in the beauty salon waiting for her to finish, I went for a walk around the shopping mall.

As I walked along looking at all of the window displays and the people, I noticed a penny on the sidewalk. Something told me to pick it up, and as I did, I got the strongest urge to pray for my own father, who had passed over due to a logging accident when I was a preteen. Praying for my father, or anyone else, at that moment was the furthest thing from my mind. I was in a shopping mall on the sidewalk.

I thought about that for a moment, then walked to the edge of the sidewalk and thought to myself, "I am going to pray for my father." I had prayed for him many times before. I do not know if he ever committed a sin in his lifetime, but I didn't think so. I had never even heard him use profanity in any form. But then, there were ten of us kids, so maybe late at night behind closed doors he expressed some frustrations in terms I never heard.

As I stood at the edge of the sidewalk looking just above the tallest palm fronds across the street, I began to meditate with my eyes open. Soon I was in a state of mind that allowed me to begin my prayer to contact him. Nothing around me disturbed me. I had cut out all outside noise.

I now concentrated on contacting the Lord Jesus Christ, and asked him over and over again to contact me. I held that found penny in my hand and could still feel that urging sensation to contact my father. My thoughts were zeroed in on making contact with the Lord Jesus Christ. Then the Lord Jesus Christ became visible to me. I asked him if my father was at Home with God. He said, "Yes, he is here, as well as Halter, Pitt, Olga and Margaret (my two uncles and two aunts) and others." Before I could ask who the others were, my father appeared and said, "I am Home and very happy." I then saw the other four, but no one else. I assume the other four were Halter, Pitt, Olga and Margaret, but they looked very young and I do not really remember what they looked like. They all looked to be at peace. Then as quickly as the Lord Jesus Christ, my father, and the others had appeared to me, they were gone. I wanted to talk to my father but did not get a chance. I did not want them to go. I could not get them back. They were gone. It was over.

My meditation and prayer were over, but I stood looking at the skyline above the palms for a short time, then slide that penny into my pocket and returned to the beauty salon where my wife was still being administered the manicure and pedicure. I felt the greatest peace in the world upon me. I felt like shouting to everyone I saw, "Be happy," but I didn't.

As I sat waiting for her with a magazine in my hands, my thoughts were centered on the event that had just taken place. Was the penny lying on the sidewalk really meant for me to pick up? I had felt such a strong urge to pick it up that I just had to. I had heard of this before as being a sign from a loved one who had passed over trying to send a message or reminder that they were there watching over you. I wondered if it would have been the same if that penny had been a $100 bill. I think people would have been fighting over that bill but not the penny. I have seen many people walk by a penny on the sidewalk without giving a thought to picking it up, myself included. Why did that particular penny attract me and urge me to pick it up?

That evening while we were sitting around the dining room table, a bell rang three times from our son's bedroom. He has a bell like those used in stores for customers to tap on the top which alerts the store clerk that they need assistance. There is nothing near the bell that would cause it to ring. Something would have to fall on it or hit it. Nothing like that happened or could have taken place. We have thought that possibly that was some kind of signal to us from the other side that all was well.

The Indian Burial Ground

When my wife was 13 years old she accompanied her family to a northern California community to visit friends. While there, the family was shown several large buckets of what the friend described as Indian beads he had removed from Indian gravesites. He told my wife that she could have some of them, so she scooped a handful from one of the buckets and placed it in a small bag. She was told that she could make bracelets and necklaces with them. She took the bag home and placed it in a drawer, never thinking much about it anymore. She kept the bag in her nightstand, knowing what it was and just kept it in a safe place.

One day 23 years later, she happened to look into the bag, which by now was stored in a jewelry box. She told me what it was and asked if I would like to see them. She related the story of how she had acquired those items. I said that I would like to look at them, but

I really did not feel right about them being taken from an Indian burial ground and now being in her possession. There were beads and some teeth.

We discussed the fact that these artifacts were from sacred Indian burial grounds and that it was belief of the Indians that these grounds were holy and should not be disturbed. We determined that we would return them to a reputed Indian burial ground near where we lived at that time – Pahrump, Nevada.

We carefully took the bag of artifacts and drove to the location. We picked a spot near the base of a sage bush. We said a prayer for whoever they were, asking the Lord to take the spirits in the artifacts into His domain, Heaven. We then prayed to the Lord and to the spirits to forgive my wife for having them in her possession because she did not know it was a violation of their sacred beliefs.

It was a cool, still evening. As we completed the prayer and began depositing the artifacts back to the Earth onto the burial location, a very slight breeze blew across us, and my wife swears that on that very slight breeze was a clear and audible whisper, "Thank you." The slight breeze lasted only a moment, and that was while we were returning the artifacts back to the Earth.

My wife asked me, "Did you hear that?"

I said, "I heard nothing." Our son was present and he heard nothing.

To this day, we occasionally drive to that location, stop, and say a prayer. On a few of these occasions my wife has received a whispered, "I love you," always accompanied by a momentary slight breeze. I have never heard the whisper, but have felt the breeze.

Interestingly enough, there is a well-known, upscale restaurant nearby, and since that date we returned the artifacts to their rightful place, there has been a friendly ghost seen on the stairways in the restaurant by many of the employees. No one there is frightened by it. It has become routine to those who work at that restaurant.

A UFO Flew over Pahrump, Nevada

Late one night (about midnight) in early 1997 my wife and I were sitting up talking and listening to the police scanner, as there was always quite a bit of police action in Pahrump at night because people habitually exceed the 35 mph speed limit, especially drivers from out of state or those who have been drinking. There are always the usual DUIs, expired plates, no seat belts, drugs and things like that.

This night was different. An excited deputy sheriff who was on patrol, came on the scanner. He said, "Sarge, look up in the sky just above the Mountain View (a casino). Look at that. What is it?" The sarge came on and said in a very stern voice, "Keep your eyes on the road. Don't look up. Keep your eyes on the road and stay on patrol. Stay on patrol." The deputy responded, "Yes sir."

We made our way out of our home to see what the deputy was referring to. There it was. It was a huge, slow moving object about 500 to 750 feet above the ground. It was moving in an easterly direction at no more that 15 miles an hour. It was circular in shape and had two sets of very bright blinking lights that circled the outer edge of the craft in opposing directions. The lights were a variety of colors – bright white, yellow, green, blue and red.

This craft had a propulsion system. We could hear it. It was a low, muffled, smooth sound. It flew by us at a distance of 1,000 feet. The craft was not an airplane. It was not a helicopter. Nor was it a blimp. There are military and commercial aircraft and helicopters over this area many times a day. We were unable to identify the sound of its propulsion system.

There was no mention of this event in our local newspaper or other media. We talked to a friend of ours who at that time was working in a big gold mine near Tonopah, Nevada. He just laughed and said that was nothing compared to the things he had seen very close up many times at night near the place where he worked, which borders a secret government installation called Area 51.

Area 51 does not exist on any official government documents, nor is it on any maps. It is there and does exist notwithstanding these exclusions and denials. This is a huge area. Anyone who should foolishly stop along the highways that pass through it or border it, and cross the first barbed wire fence (clearly marked that deadly force will be used past that point) will have a surprise. They will be met by either armed patrols or helicopters, and have any cameras, tape recorders or other electronic instruments they may be carrying taken from them. They will be arrested and taken to an interrogation center for questioning before they are released or charged with trespassing.

There is also a second barbed wire fence. Don't cross that one. If you should cross that second fence, the patrols shoot on sight and shoot to kill. This area is surrounded by Nellis Air Force Base Test Range, Nevada Nuclear Test Site (almost 1,000 nuclear bomb detonations took place there), Groom Lake and an area called S-4. What goes on in these locations is of the utmost national security. We are probably a free society today because of these and other such secret areas strategically located throughout the country.

I believe that our government does have secrets, and that these secrets should not be divulged to the general public. The devices developed and tested there would most likely scare the pants off most people. But they are being developed and designed for the security of our nation and our way of life. We cannot tell other nations or organizations (our enemies) what goes on there. These areas are so secret that those who have worked there in certain capacities on certain projects, cannot prove they ever worked there.

Those who presently work there and those who have worked there all sign a nondisclosure agreement swearing that they will never divulge any information to anyone regarding their work, what they saw or heard.

Men in Black

I have had several people come to me with stories of men in black. Each of these stories are similar. They all have occurred in the same area. The sighting was a line of men walking through the desert near the secret area. They were about one mile from the observers. These men were all dressed in black business suits and walked single file. They had human characteristics and walked with the average gait of a human. They walked to a mountainside and then into it without hesitation. There was no visible sign of any entrance where they could do that. They simply walked into the mountain.

I was required by all of them to clearly understand that I did not have their permission to use their names – only their experience. These are all respected and well-educated people.

I have also heard tales of people who have witnessed what appeared to be large aircraft and saucer-shaped craft fly into mountains at high rates of speed where there was no visible entrance for them.

I have included these stories because EHMR suggested that I do so. He did not tell me why I should do this, but I think it is to show a relationship between the natural world that we live in during our natural lives and the supernatural world (spiritual) where we live upon our departure from this life.

CHAPTER 16
MY NEW CONTACT

My wife and I were visiting her parents in Southern California in 2001 after she visited one of her doctors. She had another doctor appointment for the next day, so we stayed overnight at her parents' home. It was a very pleasant and casual evening. We sat around discussing current events and family as well as reminiscing on the good times. There was nothing out of the ordinary.

I went to bed that evening with my mind on our schedule for the next day. I was sleeping soundly when I was awakened at about 2 o'clock in the morning by a bright light in the room. I sat up in bed and looked around, but there was no one there. The room was brilliantly lit. There were no lights on in the bedroom. I knew what was going to happen though, and got out of bed. I stood beside the bed for a few moments looking at my wife sleeping. This brilliant light did not awaken her, and neither did I.

Shortly, EHMR appeared. He was not alone. Previously he had always appeared to me alone, even though at our first meeting there were other aliens present in the craft that I boarded. None of the others communicated with me, and I did not see their faces because they all had their backs turned toward me.

This time was different. I could see the face of this new entity. This was the first time I had seen the face of any alien other than EHMR. He looked much different than EHMR and did not match the pictures I had seen or the descriptions given by others of aliens. He appeared to be a male. There was a golden hue to his body, and there was a ruby colored beam emanating from his eyes onto me. To describe him is very difficult. His features were chiseled and he had short, semi-curly hair. He was handsome. He was more than handsome – he was beautiful in a very manly sense. He appeared to be powerful and strong, resembling that of a statue of an ancient Greek god. When I use the words "handsome and beautiful" in describing this entity, I want you to know that I have never seen a handsome man or an ugly woman in my life. I just do not have any other words to describe him.

EHMR and the new entity stood looking at me for several moments without saying anything. I had no fear of this new entity. I was familiar with EHMR, and he had assured me many times that there would be no harm come to me, but nothing could surprise me either. EHMR never has a "hello," "goodbye," "have a nice day," or "good luck" at these meetings.

EHMR said, "This is your new contact. From this day forward I will no longer be contacting you. You will be contacted by your new handler." I waited for EHMR to continue – make some kind of introduction, but he just stood there waiting for me to say something. Finally I asked EHMR where he was going. I waited, expecting him to say that he had fallen down on his duties or something like that. He responded to me by informing me that I was not to concern myself with that, because that was just the way it had been determined that this was going to be; the way things are done. He stated that this would not interfere with or change the mission I had accepted.

I asked him why I was assigned a new handler, because I was familiar with and trusted him. Now I would have to concern myself with a new handler. I told him that I needed to know this; and also where he was going. He responded that my new handler was his superior, and from that day forward I would be contacted by my new handler.

I realized that I was not going to find any answers to my questions

– at least at this time. All during this time, the new entity stood silent and calm, looking at me. I then said to EHMR, "I have known all along that there were things that you would not or could not tell me, and I assume this must be one of those." I told EHMR that I would continue the mission as I had promised.

EHMR then said to me, "You are now beginning to understand. You are willing to complete this mission, and it will not change. You have much to learn." He went on to say that his duties were to make initial contact with people willing to perform this mission. He stated he had given me training and assistance and that he was now satisfied with my progress, and it was time for a higher authority to assist me. He said he was going to be doing something else, and that was all I needed to know about him.

I now realized that there really was a hierarchy in EHMR's world. He reiterated to me then, that my mission would remain the same. I told him that my mission had been for him – that I did not know there would be someone else. He reminded me that he had made reference many times to "we," and he had always meant more than just himself. I recalled that, but I had always thought within myself that it would always be just EHMR. He asked me if I still wanted to continue with the mission that I had promised I would perform. I said yes. He then said that is the way it will then be, and I must work closely with my new handler. *Here is that word "handler" again,* I thought to myself. So I asked him, "Is there a difference between a handler and a contact?" EHMR responded that the meaning was the same, that it was just in my own mind as to how I should perceive the meaning.

EHMR then said they were going to depart, and asked if there were any further questions I had at that time. I told him, "Yes there is. What is my new handler's name?" He would not tell me what his name was. Instead he said that it was not important for me to know that, and he was not going to go into that. He said that would be at the discretion of my new handler to divulge that information when he determined it was necessary and appropriate.

He went on to say that he had shown me the proper way to use the numbers of humans, and that my new handler was many steps above himself on the ladder. He told me that my new handler would always be nearby and would contact me when he felt it was necessary and would let no harm come to me or my family. I only needed to concentrate on my mission because it would be very rewarding to me as well as many, many others.

At one time my wife asked me if I would awaken here when EHMR showed up. I told her that I would. *Well,* I thought, *I am going to ask EHMR if I can awaken her so she can see and meet him and the other entity.* I asked him if I could awaken her. He told me that I could not do so because it was not time for her to meet them. He informed me that there is a set time in the future for her to meet them and she will be offered a mission. He stated that she already knew who they were and had been given many gifts. She is being prepared to meet them but does not realize it, nor does she know the source of those gifts.

EHMR said he would no longer be in contact with me. They then departed. They just vanished as did the bright light. I was standing alone now with only the light from the outside street lights faintly illuminating the room.

I could make out the vague figure of my wife sleeping. I went to the door, opened it quietly and looked down the hallway to the family room. It was dark. There was no one out there. Everyone was asleep. I returned to the bed and as I sat down my wife awakened and asked me where I was going. I said, "I think I just got back." She sat up in bed, and I related the event that had just taken place. We discussed this for a while.

She asked me more questions than I had asked EHMR. I did not tell her they did not want her to meet them yet.

We talked about the new entity. We tried to figure out who he might be in the hierarchy of the spiritual realm. We discussed and tried to figure out why he would not divulge his name. I recalled that EHMR had told me on several occasions the he did not have a name as humans do. They are called by what they do. He does not have a name – he has a title which describes what he does. That title is who he is. The dilemma here was what were we going to call this new entity?

We decided we would call him Mr. No Name. This is not out of disrespect. We simply did not know what other name would be appropriate. He was EHMR's superior. Who is he? We may find out eventually, but right now I needed a name for him.

The realization hit me that I had just met another alien. This alien was more important than EHMR in the hierarchy of the spiritual or dimensional realm. He left me standing here in the bedroom without saying a word or communicating a single thought to me when he departed. There was no communication whatsoever. He was now my new contact (or handler). Somehow, I felt that this was more important than meeting EHMR for the first time.

I tried to get back to sleep. My head was spinning with questions for which I had no answers. I began wondering if this had really happened. I had met with EHMR many times and had grown used to him. I did not even consider it unusual to meet with him. I had no fear of him at all. I wondered to myself, *Was this really a new contact? EHMR said that he would no longer be in contact with me. Was he gone forever?* That made me feel sad, like losing contact with someone you know well. I knew this whole thing would take some time for me to adjust to. I determined I would continue to get this book complete.

We got up the next morning and after visiting with my wife's family for a short time, we set off for our visit with the doctor. We said nothing to her family about that visit by two aliens that night. There was no mention of a disturbance during the night. We completed the visit with my wife's doctor and then set off on the 300-mile journey back home to Nevada.

CHAPTER 17
MR. NO NAME'S SECOND VISIT

I was having quite a bit of difficulty establishing an order for this book. I would write a chapter and it was not right. I would start all over, and that wasn't right. It was a jumble. It seemed as though each time I sat down to write, there was a block.

Recalling that EHMR had told me that I was to write this book using the simplest of form and I must do it all by myself without the help of others, placed me in a quandary. Furthermore, I could only use the information he had authorized me to use. I knew I had to write all of this myself, but could I ask someone for advice as to the structure? I had to really give this some thought, serious thought. I determined that I would seek the advice of some friends whom I was certain would be willing to help with the book's structure. I determined I would do that when I had completed the rough draft of the book, but first I would have to inquire if they would help.

It was now less than a month since I had last talked with EHMR and had been shown my new contact. I was sitting at my computer that afternoon doing some writing on this book and thinking about the new contact. I had not heard a thing from him. I was thinking to myself that maybe it had all been a mistake, or a misunderstanding on my part, that EHMR was gone forever. It was during the time that I was thinking about that when I felt a "presence" near me. I knew that feeling. I was about to receive a visit. I do not know where he came from, or how long he had been there, but when I looked up and turned my head, there he was, right beside me. His sudden appearance startled me. It was not EHMR. It was my new contact, Mr. No Name.

He did not say hello to me – no greeting at all. He sat down in a chair next to my computer desk. He looked exactly the same as he did when I first saw him. He had the same golden glow from his body and his eyes looked directly at me with the same ruby colored beam. All of the time I had contact with EHMR he never sat down during my presence.

Here now, Mr. No Name was sitting in a chair in my home. I sat staring at him. He wasted no time getting directly to his purpose. He said he was now going to impart nine things to me that would assist me in my mission. Without words he transmitted those nine things to me. I could tell when he did that. I knew what they were and I knew they were from him.

I wanted to know if he had any other people like me doing a mission. I asked him, "Do you have any others here on Earth that you contact?" He said that he only contacts those who EHMR had already contacted and received promises from. Most of those have placed limits on what they will do. Some of them are wealthy and influential, while others hold positions of influence but will not step forward for fear of ridicule. They are good humans and enjoy good reputations as well as prestige and comfort. They help in ways that will not expose them to any possible ridicule. He stated that his main concern was for those humans who were willing to come forward and publicly assert and convey his message that all humans must rehabilitate themselves so that their souls may return Home upon completion of their journey of life on Earth. He stated that no human should be rejected if they have a sincere desire to help get this message communicated.

He also advised me that I must beware of people who claim they have had contact with himself and EHMR. I should use the gifts I have been given and I will know them. Further, I am to turn no one away, nor am I to ignore anyone who has questions.

I determined that I would ask Mr. No Name about the Roswell incident, even though I had asked EHMR about this and he had given me some information. I asked, "Did the Roswell, New Mexico, incident, which is reputed to have been an alien craft with aliens aboard, occur?"

He replied that there was a craft that had an accident in Roswell, New Mexico, but EHMR had already given me the answers to that question.

I told him that I felt the real facts of the Roswell incident were far from being resolved, especially in my own mind, and that I would like to know some other things that I felt were very important to my mission. I asked him, "Can the craft you travel in crash?" He said he would explain that to me, and that I could use this information in my book.

He said that there are two types of UFOs. One is observable by humans. These craft are from the same dimension in which humans exist and are from our own and other galaxies or solar systems within our universe. These can and do crash. The occupants are an intelligent life form similar, but different, than humans on Earth. Humans are attempting to solve the mysteries of space and time travel, but are limited by their material form, just as there are limitations on the UFOs we see here on Earth from within our own universe.

He told me that the other type of spacecraft and aliens are of his own dimensions. Humans are incapable of seeing any of these unless they manifest themselves to us at their discretion. They do manifest themselves to us in the forms that they determine are appropriate. They do not look anything like what I have perceived them to look like, and it is not my privilege to see them in their true dimensional form yet. That may come with time.

He told me that the craft I have seen is in the form they have manifested to me. These craft cannot crash. It is impossible. The craft I had been taken aboard are in fact a living soul which provides spiritual nourishment to all of those I observed on those craft. They are on Earth performing the missions they have been assigned by their superiors. They are here only to redeem our souls. They have no other purpose. They do not cause harm to anyone. He told me that this was all he was going to tell me on this subject.

I knew I was not going to get any further information from him on this subject, but I did want to know if he had a name. I told him that it was very difficult to refer to him only as my new contact, and asked him if he had a title or name. He said that names were not important to him, only to humans. He told me that I could not refer to him by a title. He was simply EHMR's superior and was on a much higher plane than EHMR is on, and there is no envy or resentment.

I then asked him if I could refer to him as Mr. No Name because I needed more than just a reference to a "contact" in order to express myself in this book. He said it was okay for me to do that if I so wished, and from this day forward I shall refer to him as Mr. No Name.

I asked him then if he would tell me who or what is responsible for crop circles, animal mutilations, abductions, medical experiments and such other phenomena. He told me that he was not going to involve himself in that because it is within the responsibility of humans to figure that out, and humans must strive to develop their minds. He said humans are faced with solving a great mystery, the mystery of the universe, and are waiting around for the answer to unfold before them. This will not happen until each of us realizes the purpose for which we are here, and what we must each do to return Home.

He then told me that he was departing, and that I must persevere in my mission. As quickly as he appeared, he was gone.

CHAPTER 18
REALITY

I continued struggling along on the book. It was slow going and confusing to me. I put it aside because I was having a mental block. Nothing was really making sense to me, at least in a form that I could convey the events and message of the mission I had undertaken.

We had moved to Lake Havasu City, Arizona. It was hot there, but was a beautiful setting overlooking the lake. In the evenings after the sun had set, we would sit on the patio talking and watching the stars. There was a large never-developed or improved vacant property adjoining our backyard. It gave us a clear view all around us.

One evening while sitting on the patio at about 10 o'clock, just talking casually about UFOs, extraterrestrial beings and our daily lives, with a bright almost full moon shining, Mr. No Name appeared to me. He was standing about 30 feet away from us at the edge of the large vacant property adjoining our own. I felt certain my wife and son could see him. I looked at them, but they gave no indication that they had. My wife was staring at the other side of the vacant lot as though watching something. I could see nothing where she was looking. I said nothing. Just sat there looking at Mr. No Name.

He said nothing either. He just stood looking at us. This went on for a few minutes but I don't know how much time passed, then he was gone. There had been no communication whatsoever. He had just looked at us. There were no shadows or trees that could have cast that image, because there were none around.

I looked at my wife and she was now looking at me. I wondered if she had seen what I had just seen, but she made no mention of anything, except she had a rather puzzled look on her face. We resumed talking about the moon and stars, but real soon agreed to go into the house.

Our son went to bed. It was also time for us to retire for the evening, but when we got to the bedroom I closed the door and asked her if there was something she wanted to ask me. I said I had seen a puzzled expression on her face just before we came into the house, and that she appeared to be transfixed on a particular spot in the vacant lot.

She said that she had just seen a ghost-like young couple merrily dancing in the vacant lot. They were dancing in a circular motion that took them onto the street and then back onto that vacant parcel of land. They did not seem to be bothered by the ditch between the street and the parcel, or the rough terrain of the parcel. They appeared to be floating just above the surface, as though on an invisible dance floor.

They were happy and smiling at each other. The young lady wore an ankle length dress that flared outward when she whirled, and the young man was dressed in what appeared to be a tight fitting leather-like suit. The clothing was neat but appeared to be old-time, similar to depictions of clothing from about a thousand years ago. The time of the Druids came to her mind.

She was mesmerized while that event was playing out. She said they danced and whirled around and around oblivious to anything around them. They did not look at us, just kept smiling and looking at each other. They appeared to be deeply in love. They then faded away.

I told her that I had been visited by Mr. No Name at the same time she was experiencing her observation of the two ghostly dancers. We discussed the fact that I had not seen her dancers and she had not seen Mr. No Name.

We talked of many stories residents in Lake Havasu City relate about seeing apparitions on or near the most famous landmark in Lake Havasu City – the London Bridge. There are visitors from all over the world coming here just to walk across the bridge and see it. There are visitors, as well as local residents, who claim to have seen apparitions of Druid-like figures strolling across the bridge late at night. We decided we would make some frequent visits to the bridge at night to attempt to see these ourselves. But, after several months of periodically doing that, we stopped with no results at all.

It was very difficult to write there. It seemed that there was no spirituality in the area. Others had confided to us that they felt the same way. I could not get in the mood to write and when I forced it, I would simply go blank. It was a real struggle.

A year before moving to Lake Havasu City, Arizona, I was walking from the kitchen in my home to the living room. Suddenly, I blacked out and collapsed onto the floor. My wife heard me fall and called 911. This blackout lasted about seven seconds and when I came out of it, I felt fine. When the paramedics arrived, I met them at the door and told them I was okay. Of course, they took my vital signs but found nothing out of the ordinary except high blood pressure.

They did suggest that I see a doctor that day, and left. As soon as they left I went into my bedroom and laid down, feeling a need for rest. As I lay there I felt a strange sensation coming over my body. It simply consumed me. I had another seven-second blackout. My wife called 911 again and this time they took me to a medical clinic. We arrived at the clinic and a physician's assistant examined me. Again my blood pressure was high but there was nothing else. While the medical personnel at the clinic were taking a history of my health, I had another seven-second blackout. They found that during these blackouts my blood pressure soared to over 210/110 and my heart rate slowed to 30 beats per minute. They put me on a Flight For Life helicopter and flew me to a Las Vegas hospital.

They thought it was my heart at first but after many tests determined it was not. MRIs and X-rays soon showed there was a small spot under the frontal lobe of my brain. The doctors determined that was the problem. They had placed me on anti-seizure medications to stop the blackouts and set me for surgery to remove the spot on my brain. I had experienced no pain or headaches prior to the seizures. There was no indication at all of any problem.

The operation was successful, and I was advised that my problem was corrected. Before I was released I had an interview with the doctor who performed the operation. He said he was curious if I had recently been exposed to any high doses of radiation or some form of potent bacteria. I advised him of two nuclear detonations in which I had been a participant, but those were years ago, and I had had no recent known exposure to radiation. I had been in no known bacterial tests. I informed him that the only thing recent that I had a problem with was a tooth which had become inflamed. I had been taking some antibiotics to clear up the infection before a dentist was going to remove it. He said that was dental, and had nothing to do with what he was talking about. It bothered me somewhat that he was looking for a source of what caused the seizures.

I asked that doctor if it would be okay if I got the tooth extracted and was assured by him that it was okay. Two weeks later I got that tooth extracted. I told the dentist about the operation I had recently undergone (my eyes were still black and my head had bandages on it). He didn't seem very interested so I did not pursue the conversation.

But a year later I had another episode with what was called a seizure. That operation was supposed to have solved that problem. Again I underwent MRIs and all of the tests. There was no sign of the tumor. They were puzzled and determined that it must be the result of having had brain surgery. I did inform those doctors of the fact that I had an inflamed tooth and was taking an antibiotic. They told me that had nothing to do with this problem of seizure because it was dental.

They placed me on a very potent medication (Dylantin) to prevent seizures. I was to take these for the rest of my life. They further instructed me to take the six 100-milligram pills daily, and that if I did not do so great harm and even death could come to me. I was told that this medication was the only thing that would prevent my seizures.

Shortly after being released from the hospital I had that abscessed tooth extracted. I dutifully took the Dylantin as instructed as well as a high blood pressure medication I had been directed to take. The Dylantin began affecting my concentration and made me feel terrible. It made me tired and lethargic. I simply could not effectively function or concentrate.

It was now necessary for me to have weekly blood tests to check the Dylantin level in my system. If the level gets too high it becomes very toxic and causes serious damage, and if it gets too low I would have a seizure. So I was in and out of doctors' offices and blood testing centers all of the time. The problem with that is that it takes so long for the lab tests to come back to the doctor's office that they are of little value because they are over a week old, if the lab should send them at all. The doctors never prescribed any correction to the dosage. But when I inquired what I should do if I felt that my Dylantin level was too low, I was told to just take more.

We moved from Lake Havasu City back to Nevada shortly after that second seizure. I was unable to effectively function there either. We stayed there for a short time and then moved to California, as we had some business matters to get cleared up there which were going to take several months. We got those matters cleared up and determined we would stay there for a while longer.

During that time, I was taken to a hospital for having too much Dylantin in my system. It was horrible. I could not walk. I had no strength in my legs or arms. They treated me for too much Dylantin in my system. A doctor, after examining all of my medical records and the records of the operation for removal of the tumor, informed me that he did not see how the tumor removal operation could be causing the seizures because the tumor was only in the fatty tissue around the brain. There was no part of the brain that was cut, and the tumor was the size of a grain of rice. I inquired what he meant by that, and he said he had no explanation – that it just puzzled him. But, he did not change the Dylantin dosage; in fact he insisted that I continue its use.

In December 2003, I had a seizure. I called the doctor and was told to just go to the hospital and he would attempt to find a neurologist to see me. His receptionist called back and informed me that because the Christmas season was near, the doctor would not be back until a week after New Year's and they were unable to locate a neurologist. I decided to stay home and not go to the hospital and get another huge bill for nothing. None of these doctors knew what they were treating me for or why they were treating me. I was just a paycheck.

I was taking the six pills per day. There should be no reason for a seizure as these pills were supposed to prevent them. There was no tumor and there was no scarring of the brain because the operation did not touch the brain – only the fatty tissue surrounding it. Why would I have a seizure? This did not seem right to me. I was also having a problem with another tooth which was causing inflammation and swelling of the gum.

I was now back to work on my obligation to get EHRM's message out by writing this book. It was January 4, 2004, when I received another visit from Mr. No Name. He had a rather terse message for me, "Get the book completed quickly." He informed me that I would write this in the way he directed and that I would include the stories that are now in here. Plus, the last story I am to relate is that of two angels who had once visited me. He went on to say that all of these stories are important, and I must include them, but did not tell me why they are important. He departed abruptly without giving me an opportunity to ask why they were important.

On the evening of January 5, 2004, I was still quite concerned about how I was going to go about this in a manner consistent with what Mr. No Name required. I determined that I would ask if he would contact me because I was having so much concern about my lethargy, exhaustion and memory. It was only moments later that he made himself visible to me. He told me that I would complete the book quickly, but he was going to tell me some things that would help me do that. He further told me that I could not reveal these things he was going to tell me. He then gave me information that shocked and stunned me. I had a difficult time accepting what he said.

This is one of the things he told me. He informed me that my exhaustion, lethargy and memory problems were the result of the medications I was taking. He told me that I was to cease taking the medication, because I was being improperly diagnosed and treated. He said that the doctors had all been mistaken in their diagnosis and what they thought was the problem was not it at all. My problem was caused by an infection in a tooth. The infection was not of concern to most doctors or dentists, and many did not even understand the seriousness of a bacterial infection deep in the roots of teeth. He informed me that such infections cause serious injury to nerves, brain and other organs as well as the joints and muscles. He stated that that infection had spread to other teeth, and when the bacteria from a tooth infection gets released into the bloodstream, it is so toxic it will cause what appears to be an epileptic seizure, heart attack and even death.

He then told me that I will go immediately to a Dr. Ihab E. Hawary,

DDS, at California Smile Design whose office is directly across the street from where I am right now, Jamboree Road and DuPont Drive in Irvine, California. He directed me to contact him immediately when I arose the following day and made an appointment to get my teeth completely fixed, and with that all of my medical problems would be resolved. He stated that Dr. Hawary would know what to do. He directed that I do that. He said it would take me a few months to recover from the effects of the Dylantin because of the damage it had done to my body and nervous system. Then I would be able to complete the book.

He reiterated that I was not to divulge any information that he had just given me to any person until such time as I was authorized by him to do so. He told me that withholding certain information from me and others was deliberate and necessary on their part. For if they were to provide all of the answers to questions we have, there would be no necessity for faith or hope. Each human receives a soul at conception and each is provided with free will. How they exercise that free will is up to each human and each human must protect their own souls. There are some things that are predetermined, but if all things in human life were predetermined, there would be no purpose for the existence of human life on Earth.

I asked Mr. No Name if he would tell me about the phenomena of a vortex. He said that a vortex (as humans call it) is an energy field established by him as an area they use as a source. That is where all things happen while they are here. Only they can create an area of this nature. Man cannot create a vortex. There are many vortexes on Earth, each created for a different purpose, and there are many purposes. A vortex is the light through which you must pass to return home, and is also the light through which souls pass when they are sent to Earth.

I asked Mr. No Name if there was a vortex at the location where I had first met with EHMR. He said there is a vortex at that location and that it will continue to exist as one. I asked him why they would have a vortex in such a lonely, isolated area. He informed me that was not to be any of my present concerns, but that many things take place in a vortex, because that is an established zone where the material world and the spiritual world can meet.

Mr. No Name then departed without any further comment.

The next morning when I awakened, I discussed that meeting with my wife. I told her that I was to contact Dr. Hawary and get all of my teeth fixed. Neither of us thought there was much wrong with my teeth. I had occasionally had a tooth pulled because it became abscessed, but no dentist had done any kind of serious evaluation. We determined however, that we would make that appointment. The most amazing part of it is that Mr. No Name designated the dentist I would visit who would correct this problem.

I was deeply concerned about what Mr. No Name had told me, because all of my doctors said that I must take that medication for the rest of my life. This was more than just one doctor; it was at least 15. Now an extraterrestrial being directs that I cease taking those medications. Most people with whom I have shared the existence of Mr. No Name and EHMR have real serious doubts about their existence, while others make no bones about what they think of their existence.

My wife, son and I are the only people I know who truly know of and believe in the existence of EHMR and his superior, Mr. No Name. I do know they exist, and because of that I determined that I would not take the Dylantin any longer. I want to be perfectly clear here – I trusted Mr. No Name, but at the same time had my doubts and fears about giving up that medication completely. It was a serious and solemn decision.

I made and kept the appointment for two days later with Dr. Hawary. I informed him that I wanted any problems with my teeth and gums to be completely taken care of at the earliest possible time.

I was given an examination, X-rays and an evaluation. He advised me what I should have done. He was very thorough. I had all of my front teeth and had only lost some molars. Dr Hawary informed me that there was an infection in the roots of some of my teeth and it had gotten into the bone. There was one especially troublesome lower front tooth that, even though it looked healthy, had an infection in the root.

When he began pulling it, he ran into a great deal of difficulty. It did not want to come out. Generally, the front upper and lower teeth are simple to pull and are removed easily. This was much different. It was fused to the jawbone, as though they were one. Almost two hours later he had chipped it out of my jawbone, then treated the cavity left there and placed me on a serious 30-day antibiotic regimen to rid the jawbone of that bacterial infection. In 30 days the bacterial infection was gone.

I do not take the Dylantin, and I do not need it. But, with the constant memory of all of those previous doctors before and their warnings, I still carry a little pack of that medication in my pocket wherever I go.

Since that time I have found, through research and investigation, that the original seizure I suffered and all subsequent seizures, were not caused by that little benign brain tumor or a heart problem. It was caused by a bacterial infection in my teeth. If that bacteria should get into your bloodstream in even the most minute amounts, it may cause you to have seizure-like episodes, heart problems, and problems with your other organs and joints. It can kill you. I went through three years of hell, and it amazes me that an extraterrestrial being had to tell me what was wrong. I am really glad I listened to him! I seriously urge each person to pay special attention to their dental health even if you feel there is no problem. Many health problems are caused by dental problems and are never detected by the regular medical doctor, because a dental problem is not their field of medicine. They simply ignore it, and now that you are in their office, they are going to treat you for something even if they do not know what it is. They will make up stories that will knock your head off and deplete your pocketbook. They do not truly care about you; they are after as much of your money as they can dig out of you.

I got my dental work all done and feel better than I ever have. I thank Dr. Hawary for his expert and professional abilities and recommend him to anyone in need of competent dental care. Dr. Hawary has an excellent staff well-trained in state-of-the-art dentistry. They are all professional. My special thanks goes to two of Dr. Hawary's staff, Chetna Worlikar and Lucia Andrade. I urge any person who has any kind of dental problem to contact a competent, caring dentist.

I was reinvigorated. I determined that I would complete this book and began earnestly doing so and for the first time in a long time began enjoying it.

I completed the book but without any of the information Mr. No Name had given me at that January 5, 2004, meeting which included this story. I really wanted to include this dental story in this book, but recalling what I had been told – do not divulge this to anyone without prior permission – did not. This is only one of the pieces of information he had given me. I decided that I would contact him, if possible, and request his permission to include this story about Dr. Hawary and my teeth.

I made contact and requested that I be permitted to discuss this with two acquaintances of mine, Richard and Kate Mucci, the owners of "Music, Mind and Matter" (a book and music store in Pahrump, Nevada) as well as the hosts of the popular and rapidly expanding TV show *Out There*, which he gave me permission to do.

He did not at that time give me permission to divulge this to any other persons except Richard and his wife Kate. He told me that I should pay close attention to what Richard told me. I also was given a deadline in which I was to visit Richard with this request. I called Richard and made an appointment to see him.

My deadline was April 1, 2004. I visited Richard before April 1, and he listened to this story and told me that I should include this in the book. Before I could do so, however, I had to contact Mr. No Name again. I did and was told that I could now include this in the book and that I did well to consult with Richard, for he is a wise man. His TV show, *Out There*, was very important. Furthermore, I was to inform Richard that he was to persevere with the show.

The last story I was told to include in this book, is about the two angels I had met some years before. Here it is:

I know I have two guardian angels. Seven years before I met my wife I was visited by two angels one evening. I had just got into bed when they appeared above me at what seemed a long distance away. The ceiling in the bedroom was only eight feet high. It looked like they were approaching me through a cone of light which enveloped me. One of the angels had black hair said her name was Lila, and introduced the other angel, who had golden hair, as Julie. Julie never spoke.

They approached very close to me, and Lila said to me, "We are now going to show you the one. You will take this woman to be your wife." They showed me a beautiful woman and said I would know her when I saw her. Lila floated down and kissed me on the left check. The two angels and the beautiful woman then faded away.

I thought this was probably the strangest thing I had ever encountered, at least up to that point. And I thought about that many times thereafter. The image of that woman, and the encounter, were indelibly printed on my mind, and it would not fade away. I have seen my two guardian angels since that time on several occasions.

One day seven years later, I was at a fast food restaurant having lunch when two ladies sat down at the booth beside me. I paid no attention to them. They were discussing a situation that involved a real estate transaction and were going to try to locate a real estate company but were not familiar with any. I was in the real estate business part-time and asked if they would pardon my interruption. I gave them my card and said that I might be of some assistance in handling the sale of the property or that I might be able to direct them to someone who could help.

When I saw that lady's face, I knew instantly she was the one who my guardian angels had shown me. Everything about her was exactly the same. I assisted her in dealing with the real estate transaction, but to make a long story short, we are married now.

When I first became involved with the "presence" and the "voice" I was certain I was dealing with aliens from our own dimension. I had not even thought of aliens from another dimension. There are alien life forms and mechanical devices from our own galaxy, but there are also alien life forms from other dimensions and other universes. I have become involved solely with the alien life forms from those other dimensions, and have no true knowledge of those from our own dimension except what EHMR and Mr. No Name have related to me. What they told me makes sense to me.

Who is Mr. No Name? I know he is a god, but which one is still a mystery to me. I know there is a hierarchy in Heaven (Home), and it is based on the planes of the ladder. I know there are many gods, and each has a domain. I know that EHMR and Mr. No Name are involved in the domain that is responsible for human souls returning Home, but what else they are involved in I do not know. I know there are gods whose domain is the spirits of all other animals, and that those animals return Home.

I know each person has two guardian angels which are given to them at conception. I have two guardian angels, for I have seen and met them on more than one occasion. These angels will telepathically talk to you if you just listen for them. You can also see them. They provide wonderful guidance to many.

There are also demon angels from hell, who will talk to you and mislead you, and if invited by you will take over your body and inhabit your soul. These demon angels must be invited by you. If you feel their presence, you have the power to reject them. They will destroy you if you permit them to hang around you. There are many humans possessed by demons.

At a meeting with Mr. No Name, I asked him why I had never met any aliens other than EHMR and him. I said that I had seen others on a spacecraft at the first meeting I had with EHMR, but never saw their faces. They had stood looking down into a podium-like object protruding from the floor, never moving or looking up.

He said that the aliens I had observed were souls, and they are from Home, each having a specific duty and responsibility associated with this mission I had volunteered to perform. What I had observed was the equivalent of them at a dinner table. They were receiving their nourishment from the spacecraft which is a living entity. It is alive. It is not a machine. It is a superior entity that gives all direction to all other entities within its area of responsibility here on Earth, as well as some other areas in other parts of this universe.

He said that the ceiling I had seen inside the craft was the mind of that living entity. The entire craft is alive, as are all of the craft from his dimension. He said these craft are manifested to us in the manner that will be the least stressful to us. There have been many other forms of them throughout the history of Earth. He further stated that the angels so many humans see and believe in are aliens.

He said that if humans truly accept the realm of the soul, then they would understand. Those who do not fully understand will have doubts of its existence. Even experiences of their own, or others, will not budge the doubts they have. But those who have the correct understanding and faith in God and demonstrate their faith and understanding by acts while here on Earth, can return Home. Just to profess faith will not get you there.

The strangest thing of all is that many humans think aliens, UFOs, souls, spirits, ghosts and other unexplainable phenomena are figments of the imagination. But in the range of true reality where the spiritual world merges with the material world, we are the temporary illusions, and they – the aliens, UFOs, ghosts, souls, angels and spirits – are forever ongoing, and are the only certain and permanent reality, and there is only one reality.

An alien told me that!

THE END

Printed in the United States
79040LV00002B/87